Lectin Free Diet

Complete Guide to Lectin Free Diet with Easy, Fast & Delicious Lectin Free Recipes to Prevent Inflammation, Diseases and Helps Weight Loss (with Slow Cooker Recipes and More)

© Copyright 2018 by Matthew Hill - All rights reserved.

The following eBook is reproduced below with the goal of providing information that is as accurate and reliable as possible. Regardless, purchasing this eBook can be seen as consent to the fact that both the publisher and the author of this book are in no way experts on the topics discussed within and that any recommendations or suggestions that are made herein are for entertainment purposes only. Professionals should be consulted as needed prior to undertaking any of the action endorsed herein.

This declaration is deemed fair and valid by both the American Bar Association and the Committee of Publishers Association and is legally binding throughout the United States.

Furthermore, the transmission, duplication or reproduction of any of the following work including specific information will be considered an illegal act irrespective of if it is done electronically or in print. This extends to creating a secondary or tertiary copy of the work or a recorded copy and is only allowed with an expressed written consent from the Publisher. All additional rights reserved.

The information in the following pages is broadly considered to be a truthful and accurate account of facts, and as such any inattention, use or misuse of the information in question by the reader will render any resulting actions solely under their purview. There are no scenarios in which the publisher or the original author of this work can be in any fashion deemed liable for any hardship or damages that may befall them after undertaking information described herein.

Additionally, the information in the following pages is intended only for informational purposes and should thus be thought of as universal. As befitting its nature, it is presented without assurance regarding its prolonged validity or interim quality. Trademarks that are mentioned are done without written consent and can in no way be considered an endorsement from the trademark holder.

Lectin Free Diet © Copyright 2018 by Matthew Hill - All rights reserved

Table of Contents

Introduction 7
Chapter 1: What Is The Lectin Free Diet 9
    How do Lectins and the intestinal wall affect each other? 13
    Benefits of the lectin free diet 15
    Can the Lectin Free Diet actually help you lose weight? 17

Chapter 2: Diet Plan for the Lectin Free Diet 29
    Foods that contain lectin 29
    Hulling brown rice or choosing white over brown 41
    Making your own tortillas will eliminate the lectin 45

Chapter 3: The phases of a Lectin Free Diet 47
    Phase 1 47
    Detox days 47

    Phase 2 55
    Phase 2 WEEK 1 Meal Plan 55
    DAY 1 55
    DAY 2: 56
    DAY 3 56
    DAY 4 56
    DAY 5 57
    DAY 6 57
    DAY 7 57
    Phase 2 WEEK 2 Meal Plan 58
    DAY 1 58
    DAY 2 58
    DAY 3 58
    DAY 4 59
    DAY 5 59
    DAY 6 59
    DAY 7 60

    Phase 3 61

- Phase 3 Meal Plan 61
  - *DAY 1* 61
  - *DAY 2* 61
  - *DAY 3* 61
  - *DAY 4* 62
  - *DAY 5* 62
- *Phases goal and time* 63
  - Phase 1 Cycle 64
  - *DAY 1* 64
  - *DAY 2* 64
  - *DAY 3* 64
  - Weekly list 65
  - Monthly list 65
  - Seasonal list 66

Chapter 4: Recipes For The Lectin Free Diet Traditionally Cooked 68

- *Meats and meat-based dishes* 68
  - Egg, Spinach, and Goat Cheese Breakfast 68
  - Omelets and salad 69
  - Chicken & Goat Cheese Enchiladas 70
- *Seafood, Salads, and vegetables* 73
  - Roasted Lemon Pepper Cabbage Wedges. 73
  - Low Carb Crispy Seasoned Jicama Fries 74
  - Mashed Cauliflower 75
  - Mashed Sweet Potatoes 76
  - Mashed Parsnips 77
  - Prosciutto, Sweet Potato, and Arugula Salad 78
  - Grilled Portobello Pesto Pizza Minis. 79
  - Baked Sweet Potato with Garlic and Kale 80
  - Stir Fried Shrimp with Bok Choy 81
  - Steak & Spinach Salad 82
  - Roasted Romain & Cobb Chicken Salad 83
  - Meatballs & Bok Choy salad 85
  - Orange & Salmon Salad 86
  - Kale and Serrano Ham Salad 88
  - Shrimp and Escarole Salad 89
  - Oven Fries 90
- *Pasta and rice* 92
  - Brown Butter Basil Sauce with Sweet potato Gnocchi 92

- Miracle Noodles with Pesto & Broccoli 94
- Creamy Spinach Ravioli with Basil Pesto 94
- Fettuccine Alfredo with Fresh Spring Vegetables 96

Desserts, snacks, dressings, and drinks 98
- Brussel Sprouts Chips 98
- Cinnamon Cassava Flour Pancakes 98
- Vanilla Cake in a Mug in 2-Minutes 100
- Basil Pesto 101
- Black Forest Cupcakes 102
- Lectin Free Blueberry Fools 104
- Ginger Cake with Cinnamon and Cream Cheese Frosting 105
- Peach Cobbler Pancake 108
- Arugula-Thyme Pesto 110
- Cilantro-Parsley Pesto 110
- Sage Pesto 111
- Minty Dessert Pesto 112
- Warm Gingerbread in a Mug 113
- Strawberry Short Cake 114
- Green Smoothie with Ginger & Mint 116

Soups and Stews 118
- Cream of Celery Soup 118
- Pork and Pineapple Stew 119
- Butternut Squash Soup 122
- Slow Cooker Sausage and Zucchini Stew 124
- Bone Broth 124
- Cream Soup 126
- Best Ever Lectin-Free Chili 127

Meats and Meat-based dishes 130
- Keto Bombay Sloppy Joe on Low Carb Buns 130
- One Pot Cranberry Apple Chicken & Cabbage 132
- Mango Chicken Thigh Sweet & Sour 133
- Lemon and Coconut Chicken 135
- Buffalo Chicken Dip With Celery Crockpot Meal 137
- Spicy Black Bean Taco Cs 137

Seafood, salads, and vegetables 141
- Prosciutto-wrapped Asparagus Canes 141
- Smothered Cajun Greens Recipe 142
- Braised Kale and Carrots 143
- Eggplant & Olive Spread 144
- Butternut Apple Mash 146

- Steamed Artichokes 147
- Mashed Acorn Squash 148
- Savoy Cabbage with Cream Sauce 149

Pasta and rice *151*
- Cajon Sausage Risotto 151
- Eggplant caponata appetizer 152

Desserts, snacks, and drinks *153*
- Pressure Cooker Applesauce 153
- Paleo Yogurt 155
- Candied Chickpea Cajun Trail Mix 156
- Classic Hummus 158
- Paleo Banana Bread 159
- Coconut Milk Yogurt 161
- Strawberry-Balsamic Sauce 163

Conclusion **165**

Introduction

Congratulations on downloading *Lectin Free Diet* and thank you for doing so.

Lectin is a potentially harmful protein that will bind to cell membranes and can be the leading cause of autoimmune disorders. When you consume lectin in large quantities, you can potentially be causing yourself more harm than good. It attached to the glucose and be the cause he bodies to hold on to those by forcing it to store them as fat. Lectin has been the contributing factor that is causing health concerns for those who have diabetes, autoimmune disorders, rheumatoid, Crohn's, irritable bowel syndrome and fibromyalgia. To have a chronic condition means that your gut is not healthy. When your gut isn't healthy, you develop chronic conditions. When we fix our gut, we fix our health.

A few key factors to consider about gut health:

- Lectins can potentially harm you. They can cause inflammation.
- Lectins help us gain weight by binding to the glucose.
- Lectins are a protein that is designed by plants to keep bugs from eating them. It works by making the bugs sick when they eat the plant stems and leaves.
- Cardiologists recommend that eliminating lectins from our diets will help us with our weight loss as well as our overall health.
- Not all Lectins are bad, some are found in healthy foods as well, such as vegetables, grains, nuts, seeds, and beans.
- Science has proven that our body cannot process lectins properly. So why eat it?
- Lectins are found in foods that are inflammatory such as squash, tomatoes, nuts, beans, whole grains, and animal proteins.

- When you eliminate the lectin in your diet, science has proven that it decreases inflammation, increases your weight loss, and improves your overall lifestyle and health.

This book has been designed to give you the ins and outs of Lectins and how going lectin free will help improve your health and lifestyle. In this book, you will find all the details you need to start the lectin free diet and advice on what you can and cannot eat. You will also find that there are several recipes and meal plan ideas to help you be successful with this diet plan.

Researchers are continuing to find new documentation on how Lectins are affecting us. There is also research that has proven the effectiveness of removing Lectins from your diet. So why are you still eating them?

There are plenty of books on this subject on the market, thanks again for choosing this one! Every effort was made to ensure it is full of as much useful information as possible, please enjoy!

Chapter 1: What Is The Lectin Free Diet

A few key factors that you should know about lectin in your life.

- Lectins have the potential to insight inflammation as well as weight gain. The lectin protein is produced by plants to insight stomach pains when they eat the plant's stems or leaves.
- Cardiologists recommend a diet with fewer lectin-based foods in it. This will improve the overall health of the dieter.
- Not all lectins are bad. However, the ones found in vegetables, grains, nuts, seeds, and beans are the worst.
- A few of the vegetables that are high in lectins are squash and tomatoes. Many of the nuts, beans, and whole grains that we consume on a daily basis can be harmful due to the high content of lectin. Another source of lectins that can be harmful is animal fats and proteins. This can be dairy, meat, and cheese.
- With all the fad diets on the market, it is hard to know what exactly people should be eating. However, it has been proven that lectin is not healthy for our body, because our bodies cannot process them.
- Plants use lectin to discourage bugs from eating them by making the bug sick, so I can only imagine what it would do to our bodies. Since humans were not designed to ingest lectins and digest them properly. It has been causing this rise in autoimmune disorders and contributing to weight gain. By removing the lectins from our diet, we are better able to maintain our health.

What exactly are Lectins?

Proteins are beneficial to our diet and health. However, not all proteins can be beneficial. Certain types of proteins, such as lectins, can bind to cell membranes and create a binding agent that helps molecules stick together. This process bypasses the use of the immune system for binding molecules.

Our immune system works to provide cell to cell interactions. These interactions can be bypassed when lectins are in high quantity. Sugar or glucose is another protein that can bound by the lectins. As they bind together, they produce a glycol or glycoconjugates on the membranes.

By binding to carbohydrates, they help the cells interact and communicate with each other. When people try to digest lectins, they receive the same type of stomach upset that is present in bugs when they are eating the plants that produce them.

Lectins bind to carbohydrates, and this helps the cells interact and communicate with each other. Lectin helps plants protects themselves from being eaten. They help by making insects and animals sick when they eat the plants. It causes stomach problems, and by using lectins, plants can survive against bugs. The same thing happens to humans as they eat lectins. It can bring up inflammatory responses that tend to increase weight gain as well as many other serious conditions. Some of these conditions include leaky gut as well as, irritable bowel syndrome.

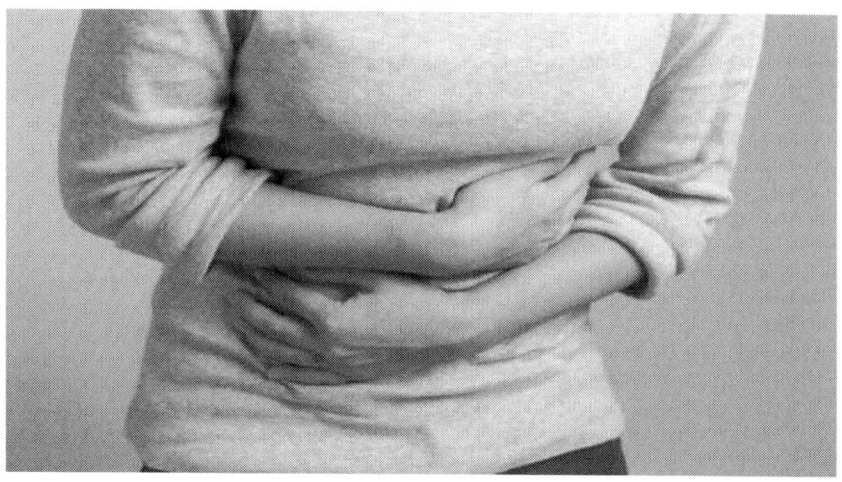

Lectins are abundantly found in raw legumes and grains. They are located in the portion of the plant that is called the seed. Seeds eventually become leaves. Cotyledon is the process with which the legumes sprout and create the protein lectin. Lectins are also found on the coating of the seeds. Other places that they are located in is dairy products as well as certain vegetables.

When you genetically alter the plants, you create some unsteadiness in the continuity of lectin in foods. Lectins help you fight against microorganisms, insects, and pests. It is speculated that lectins evolved within plants to help the seeds remain intact while they are being digested. Due to this, lectins will enter the digestive system and enter the blood without changes.

Lectins can play an important role in the immune functions, cell death, and growth, as well as regulating body fat. Lectins are not able to be digested by our stomachs. When we consume lectin's, our body adapts by creating antibodies to help with the foreign proteins within our systems. Since everyone's body reacts differently to certain proteins, each person creates an antibody designed for their body type to counter the lectin proteins. After a gut injury or immune system change your stomach can have an intolerance to certain foods. By triggering a response, lectins can stimulate the immune system and create distress.

Due to our inability to digest lectins, some of the lectins that people consume should not be used as a dietary source. Phytohemagglutinin is the process by which lectins turn raw kidney beans into poison. When you consume raw, kidney beans that have been soaked, they can be poisonous. As little as 4-5 beans can be symptomatic. A red kidney bean roughly contains 20,000 to 70,000 units of lectin; However, a full cooked bean contains about 200 to 400 units.

Some of the benefits of certain lectins can be a decrease in disease functions. We also have a few basic functions that can be supported by beneficial lectins that we consume. One of these is cell to cell adherence, programmed cell death, as well as inflammatory modulation. Our nutritional intake is based on the amount of proteins that we consume in a day, lectins that are good can provide some of these nutrients as well as anti-nutrients.

Prior to the invention of processed foods, grains were only seen at their seasonal time. They were not a high yield agricultural crop either, so there was a minor inclusion of grains in our diets. Unrefined grains carry more nutrition to our body and provide a better option for our meals, Refined grains provide less of a beneficial option. That is why a diet high in unrefined grains is a better choice. Due to the farming advancements, which have brought an abundance of grains into supermarkets, we are able to easily find the right unrefined grains that are a healthier option. On average North Americans eat more grain-based ingredients which can include many of the items listed below.

- Bread
- Rice
- Pasta
- Cereals
- And more.

Our bodies are not designed to process the onslaught of grains in our diet. However, our ancestors found that if you soak, ferment, cook or sprout the grains you can decrease the lectins which frees up the good nutrients. Lectin yield differs from year to year in our crops.

Negative side effects of lectin in your diet and your health.

Basically, lectins can cause you to be flatulent. In some circumstances, legumes and grains, when eaten raw, can cause nausea, vomiting, and even diarrhea. It has been speculated by researchers that bacterial food poising has been contributed to lectin poisoning.

How do Lectins and the intestinal wall affect each other?

So why do we see an influx of digestive issues due to lectin? Lectins will damage the intestinal lining which causes the digestive distress. When food is passed through the gut, it will not cause any damage to the lining or GI Tract. The cells in our body are designed to repair this damage quickly. However, lectins blunt the ability to a speedy recovery. The purpose of the stomach lining is to only allow good stuff through and contain the Bad stuff that we ingest. To run at full efficiency for cellular repair, the stomach must operate in this way. Because of lectins, our body will not regenerate properly. The cell will not be able to secure the intestinal lining. This compromises our guts and can damage the intestinal stomach linings. Essentially causing our leaky gut syndromes. Leaky gut will allow various molecules to bounce around inside the gut wall. It can block the vitamins and minerals that we need. When lectin is consumed in a large enough quantity it can trigger a GI evacuation this can mean vomiting or even diarrhea.
There are a few lectins that are associated with digestive complaints more often:

- Dairy
- Cereal
- Legumes
- Grain
- Peanut
- Soybean
- Seafood

What can lectins do to the immune response?

By damaging the gut wall, you trigger the immune system response. This is our bodies defense against toxic invaders, lectins. The symptoms to look for are:

- Joint pain
- Generalized inflammation
- Skin rashes

Leaky gut has been connected to several diseases and chronic disorders. It has been stated that autistic children will be more prone to leaky gut and other inflammatory syndromes. They are also highly susceptible to GI tract issues. Those who suffer from Crohn's disease as well as, irritable bowel syndrome can have a higher sensitivity to lectins in their diet. It is possibly due to the high population of immature cell varieties. Another contributing factor could be the high turnover of cells as well. Immature cells have an abundance of locations that provide an easy attachment spot for the lectins. When we ingest the lectins, they can affect our gut lining and inflammatory conditions for the length of time they are within our body. The effects of these lectins can be reduced by eating vegetables, fruits, and beneficial bacteria's, such as fermented foods, along with the food that is high in lectins.

Benefits of the lectin free diet.

The Lectin Free diet is a "blood type diet," and it is based on how our blood cells will react to lectin that is in our foods. Experts have found a connection to the 8 most common allergens and lectin. The highest allergen contains lectins are listed below.

- Soy
- Egg
- Shellfish
- Wheat
- Tree nuts

- Peanuts
- Dairy
- Fish

Doctors have found a connection between Urinary tract infections and the consumption of foods high in lectins. It is also a well-known theory that those who suffer from anemia are found in countries that have a higher development of excess levels of lectin.

A diet free of Lectin is designed to help you reduce the lectin foods in your diet. These include such things as:

- Quinoa
- Eggplant
- Peppers
- Tomatoes
- And other nightshade vegetables
- Legumes
- Grains
- Dairy
- Conventionally raised meat and poultry
- Out of season fruits

Instead, you should eat low lectin foods like:

- Leafy greens
- Broccoli
- Asparagus
- Mushrooms
- Nuts and seeds
- Cauliflower
- Pasture raised meats
- Wild caught fish

Can the Lectin Free Diet actually help you lose weight?

By reducing the foods loaded with lectin from your diet, you can essentially see a change in your diet. Even though you are eating fewer varieties of food, you will still be consuming the right number of calories. The reduction in food intake allows you to reduce the amount of excess fat that your body is carrying. The reduction in fat intake along with foods abundant in lectins will help you lower your excess weight. When lectins bind to glucose and damage the lining of the gut, it triggers the body to hold on to the fat and glucose that we have taken in. This increases our fat storage and glucose storage. Once our bodies start to store excess amounts of fat and glucose, we begin to gain weight, however, by reducing the lectin intake, we reverse this effect. Now our body can start to use the glucose and fat that is stored for our energy source instead.

The reduction of lectins in our diet has been shown to improve the symptoms of cardiovascular disease, as well as metabolic syndrome. These conditions are caused by an increase in high blood sugar, high blood pressure, and larger quantities of body fat.

Produce should be consumed more often than not. The combination of whole grains and vegetables will provide more vitamins, fiber, and minerals. They can significantly outweigh the risks that are associated with small amounts of lectins, which can cause GI issues. The trick is that most foods that have lectin are still super beneficial with weight loss.

Several studies have linked the consumption of whole grains, beans, lentils, and chickpeas with those who have lost significant amounts of weight as opposed to those who did not consume them. As well as, success stories for patients that have suffered from IBS who eliminated many of the foods abundant in lectins, this includes starchy vegetables and beans.

Lectins, when eaten raw, are often troublesome in high quantities for those who have autoimmune diseases. Most people would not consume chickpeas and quinoa raw. However, there are other lectins that are consumed raw. By soaking your beans and grains for 12-24 hours, you can greatly reduce the number of lectins which have caused the GI distress. To peel and de-seed your nightshades, such as tomatoes, can help to eliminate the lectin in those vegetables. Many lectin abundant foods are anti-microbial and can have a potential anti-cancer property.

What are the benefits of the Lectin Free Diet?

Many scientists believe that lectin is harmful to your health, with inflammation causing agents as well as being symptomatic with those who suffer from celiac disease, diabetes, rheumatoid arthritis and inflammatory autoimmune disorders.
Research has found that wheat germ lectin may impact the immune system by raising the inflammation in your body. Long-term inflammation has been connected to some serious medical conditions which could include heart disease, cancer, and of course depression.

By following a lectin free diet, you may actually eliminate or lower the inflammation in your body. There is still research being studied to find the connections between lectin and autoimmune diseases. Because of lectins binding abilities, it makes it easier for bacteria or other toxins to cross your gut barrier, although they also have found that whole grains contain antioxidants which helps fight inflammation. Antioxidants can reduce the effects of the harmful lectins that we consume.

Food sensitivities are found in almost every person. By eliminating the consumption of lectins, we can greatly reduce our symptomatic food sensitivities. Researchers have found connections between food sensitivities and lectins, as well as gastric disease connections. This is thought to be due to the inability to digest the lectins. The lectins have a binding property, and when consuming them, they can potentially bind to the digestive tract and disrupt your metabolism, which can be damaging. Several scientific studies have shown a reduction in peptic ulcers. Lectin has been found to spike bacterial growth in your small intestines. With a higher bacterial growth, the mucous defense layer is then stripped, allowing stomach ulcers to grow. By eliminating lectin in your diet, you can avoid damage to your digestive tract.

The elimination of lectins can help you avoid potentially toxic foods. When we soak of foods prior to cooking, then cook them, we are able to avoid the toxic levels of lectins that can be associated with raw uncooked beans and legumes. Kidney beans are one of the beans that contain high levels of lectins, which can be toxic. Unfortunately, soaking the beans may not be enough to remove all the lectins in beans.

The risks that can be associated with the Lectin Free Diet.

Since eliminating foods is a major role in the lectin free diet plan, it may be quite difficult to follow for some people. This will limit a few of the nutritious foods that are abundant with lectins. Some of those lectin abundant foods that are also nutritious are vegetables, whole grains, and beans.

When consuming whole grains, you can potentially lower your risk of cancer, as well as reduce your condition of heart disease. Even though whole grains contain high levels of lectins, the beneficial benefits should far outweigh the negatives. This also rings true for fruits as well. The benefits of lowering the risks of several health conditions may actually be more important than the potential inflammatory concerns that come from the lectins contained within. Some of these conditions can be lung disease, heart disease, and cancer. When you consume more vegetables and fruits, you allow you are able to avoid gaining excess weight.

Because Vegans and Vegetarians practice a diet high in vegetables, fruits, and grains, it can be rather difficult for them to practice a lectin free diet plan. Since protein is found in many of the fruits, vegetables, legumes, and meats that are consumed in our diets, you can see how it would be difficult for them. The lectin free diet can be rather complicated for vegans, who cannot get protein through meat, to follow a diet that limits their intake of foods high in lectins. Vegans eat nuts, seeds, legumes, and whole grains as a viable protein source. These sources are high in lectins as well as dietary fiber.

By peeling your fruits and shelling your nuts and legumes, you can eliminate some of the lectins. However, you are also decreasing your dietary fiber.

Lectin free dieters would need to be able to consume foods that are lower in lectin content, and this includes pasture raised meats, and eggs. Since vegans do not consume any meat or meat-based sources, this would not be feasible for them. Many of the foods that are not allowed in the lectin free diet are healthy food options, there is a reduction in nutritional benefits. Lectin free diets can be lacking in fiber and many other calorie-based nutrients. These are nutrients that are optimal for your health.

Due to the cost of pasture-raised meat and eggs, the cost of a proper lectin free diet could be higher than the normal food budget for most households. Specialty milk, supplementals, and pasture-raised meat and eggs are a high-priced commodity in today's grocery stores.

Although there are many research studies being done on the subject, most of it is found to be in-vitro studies. These can be rather biased, so make sure that the studies and research you are reading are viable sources.

So how do you avoid the lectins in your food?
To avoid foods that contain lectin, you should avoid foods such as:

- Beans
- Legumes
- Soy
- Peanuts
- Grains
- Nightshades:
    - tomatoes
    - eggplants
    - potatoes
    - peppers
- cow's milk
- eggs

Many cow's and chickens are feed grains, such as wheat and corn. These grains contain lectin. By eating the meats and eggs that are feed through grains, you are in-turn eating the lectins. Which contains lectin. That means that eating only grass-fed meats and eggs is necessary to the lectin free diet.

You should also stay away from any processed or packaged foods that contain the ingredients listed above. Not all labels will be expressive of the lectin that is in them. Many of the processed foods that you currently purchase can be high in lectins, and you may not even know it. Many cereals contain soy-based thickeners or corn-based sweeteners.

So, is the Lectin Free Diet good or bad?

You will negatively impact your health by not including a variety of nutrients in your diet. If you eat enough foods, that contain the right amount of nutrients, then you should be able to have success with the lectin free diet. Based on your gut health, the lectin free diet can potentially be the right diet to help you get your gut under control.

A few guidelines to help you with the Lectin Free Diet:

- In order to eliminate lectin from your diet, you should avoid foods that are abundant in lectin every day.
- By using a pressure cooker to prepare your foods high in lectin, you are able to reduce the lectin levels.
- When you soak and boil beans, prior to cooking, you can reduce the lectin content in your food.
- By fermenting and sprouting your beans, you are able to lower the amount of lectin in your foods.
- Start slowly with the lectin free diet. Eliminate one item at a time until you are completely lectin free.
- Getting plenty of dietary fiber will help make the transition much smoother. Fiber is an important part of a proper diet. Eating enough of the fruits and vegetables that are high in fiber is a great way to maintain your health. Fiber supplements are another great option for keeping your fiber in check.
- Consult your doctor and dietician before starting any new diet. They will be able to help you with the transition and also determine if the lectin diet is right for you.

Should you ditch lectin all together?

There is no guarantee that stomach issues will be solved by eliminating lectin. Most Americans only get 10% of the daily recommended fruits and vegetables with their diets. When adding in whole grains, with the proper amounts of fruits and vegetables, you have a greater chance of reducing heart disease.

Lectin, found in raw beans, can be poisonous when ingested. Many of the foods we eat contain lectins. Earlier we listed all the vegetables and beans that are high in lectins.

Lectins are inflammatory and can be the leading cause of inflamed guts. When your gut gets inflamed, you get conditions such as Irritable Bowel Syndrome, Crohns, ulcers, and many others. It can also contribute to rheumatoid disorders and autoimmune disease. It only seems logical that eliminating the lectins in our diet would be the right choice to make.

How it prevents diseases such as Autoimmune, Diabetes, and others

Lectins have been known to irritate the gut which can be the leading cause of gut issues. When your gut isn't healthy, autoimmune diseases tend to develop. As well as other diseases such as heart conditions, diabetes, Crohn's and Irritable Bowel Syndrome. When you eliminate the lectins, you are able to boost your B12, iron, zinc, phosphorous, and magnesium. We are able to accomplish this by sprouting the beans before we eat them. By sprouting the beans, we are able to lower the lectin content.

Researchers recorded 102 autoimmune patients who participated in a lectin free diet. These results showed that each person had one of these conditions prior to the lectin free diet.

- Scleroderma
- rheumatoid arthritis
- Sjogren's
- Mixed Connective Tissue Disease
- Crohn's
- Colitis

After following a lectin free diet where they eliminated several of these:

- Grains
- Legumes
- Beans
- Cashews
- Peanuts

- Squash
- Nightshades
- casein A-1 dairy

Several improvements, in the biomarkers for inflammation, were shown. The study included tests that were performed every three months. These tests gave results for these biomarkers:

- High sensitivity C-reactive proteins
- Fibrinogen
- Autoimmune markers
- Myeloperoxidase
- Interleukins 6
- Tumor necrosis factor alpha

Each one of the patients adds in probiotics, prebiotic fiber, and polyphenol to supplement for the loss of nutrients. They found that out of 102 patients, 92 patients had no more autoimmune markers and inflammatory markers, after 9 months of the diet. The remaining 7 patients showed greatly reduced markers, and not one single patient was without change. It also showed that 70 of the patients were weaned off their immunosuppressants, as well as, other prescription medications, with no rebound effects at all.

> Dual reactivity is the process by which white blood cells will attack foreign and self-blood cells.

Due to dual reactivity, doctors have seen an increase in the diagnosis of autoimmune disorders. This can be contributed to several possibilities

Molecular mimicry

> *Molecular mimicry is the condition with which our toxins and foreign substances will share similar characteristics or structures of our tissues and the white blood cells get confused and attack our own tissue.*

Because of molecular mimicry, our white blood cells begin to attack not only the toxins or foreign substances but also our own tissue. This creates what we call an autoimmune disorder. This does not explain why the over 80 autoimmune disorders that have been diagnosed are not present in every single person. If our blood cells are attacking our own tissue due to molecular mimicry then essentially every single person would be diagnosed with an autoimmune disorder. If lectin is in everything we eat, and lectin causes this mimicry process then why aren't more people being diagnosed?

Dual Receptors

> *Dual receptor is a process by which our body uses the T cells to check our body with 2 scanners, the first scanner is identifying lectins as a foreign object and the second scanner is doing the same thing, only with our own tissue.*

This can activate two different types of armies of white blood cells: one attacking self and one attacking lectin. This white blood cell will then teach the rest of the immune system to attack healthy cells and tissues when it encounters the lectin. The old saying one bad apple ruins the whole bunch stands true with this scenario.

The lectin would become the trigger for the autoimmune disease. when something changes in our bodies, there is a trigger. In this scenario, the lectin is the trigger. To avoid being attacked, due to dual receptors, the best option is to eliminate the lectin. Thousands of people have experienced remission of their symptoms by changing their diet. This shows that by eliminating the lectin in our body, we eliminate the dual reactivity or dual receptors, which in turn eliminates the autoimmune disorders.

There is still more research that needs to be done to figure out why one person who eats lectin is triggered with Hashimoto's disease and one is triggered with Crohn's. We also don't know why some white blood cells have dual receptors that attack healthy tissue. What we do know is that diet control is an important aspect of healing the gut. Removing lectin from our diets is the first step. A proper diet can both cure and prevent diseases. This much has been proven by scientists. When we eliminate the lectins in our bodies, we can heal our gut and then heal our body. This helps prevent the destruction of our good tissue when suffering from an autoimmune disorder.

How it aids in weight loss.

Because lectins line the cell walls of our gut, they trigger a reaction. This reaction tells the body to hold on to the fat and glucose that has been consumed. By holding on to the fat and glucose that we consumed, we are storing them when we do not need to. Lectins trigger a reaction similar to starvation mode. When in starvation mode our body starts to store the fat and glucose so that we can maintain our health between longer periods without food.

When the lectin goes through the gut lining, it causes inflammation and inflammation promote fat storages within your abdomen. Your body does this in order to fight the foreign invasion, which it perceives due to the lectin. When you reduce the lectin, your cell walls regenerate, and the gut closes up allowing the body to stop storing fat. The lectin stops bind to insulin receptors, and the body no longer stores the fat in excess. Due to this chain reaction, weight loss takes place. This can also rejuvenate the skin, creating a youthful glow and a youthful appearance, by returning elasticity to the epidermis.

Chapter 2: Diet Plan for the Lectin Free Diet

Foods that contain lectin

There are several foods that contain lectin. Below I have listed many of them.

- Nightshade vegetables such as tomatoes, potatoes, goji berries, peppers, and eggplant.
- Dairy products which include milk and other milk-based products.
- Peanut-based products like peanut butter and peanut oil.
- All legumes, which includes lentils, beans, peanuts, and chickpeas.
- Products made with a grain such as flour, cakes, crackers, and bread.
- Squash
- Fruit that is out of season
- Corn
- Meat from corn-fed animals

The Most inflammatory foods to avoid are listed below.

You must stop consuming these foods while being on the lectin free diet.

- Gluten- which contains WGA. This is an inflammatory, and it is hard to remove from your diet.
- Casein-which is found in all dairy.

Never consume these foods

- Pinto beans
- Yeast (found in gluten-free bread)
- Carrageenan Gluten-containing grains and any grains not listed elsewhere.
- Kidney beans
- Almond milk, nut milk.
- Cashews
- Peanuts
- Various legumes

Avoid these if you are lectin sensitive

Consuming these at night is not a great idea. And if you are lectin sensitive or have an autoimmune disorder, consuming these foods would be hazardous.

- Chickpeas
- Brown rice
- Lentils
- Corn on the cob. However, do not consume this if you have severe lectin allergy.
- Basmati White rice. Starch is an important part of your diet, but if you have a sever lectin allergy do not consume them.
- Parboiled rice.
- Semi-green bananas
- Plantains
- Soaked lentils
- Taro
- Pumpkin
- Cassava
- Winter Squash
- Carrots
- Tomato
- Walnuts
- Pistachio nuts
- Skinned almonds
- Wild blueberries
- Olives
- Almonds
- Brazil nuts

Avoid these if you have any type of food sensitivity

- White potatoes
- Herring
- Sourdough bread
- Moldy cheeses
- Ripe bananas
- Whey
- Figs
- Raisins
- Sprouted buckwheat/Go Raw Granola
- Grapes
- Hummus without additives
- Chocolate/Cocoa (including raw cacao)
- **Caffeine**
- Most legumes
- Tuna
- Beta-lactoglobulin (in all dairy)
- Kefir
- Oats
- Unmodified Potato starch. Placed here because of high RS
- Buckwheat (un-soaked)
- Orange sweet potatoes

Foods that are without lectin or have a small percentage of lectin in them

Everything we eat contains a small amount of lectin. Fruits and vegetables have a lower content of lectin. The ones below are some of the lowest values of lectin:

- pumpkin
- onion

- broccoli
- mushrooms
- sweet potato
- strawberries
- carrots
- cauliflower
- asparagus
- cherries
- apples
- lemons
- blueberries
- oranges
- cherries

Animal proteins are a great option for a lectin free diet. This can include fish, beef, chicken, and eggs that are grass fed. As well as avocados, butter, and olive oils. They contain high fat and make meals well balanced and healthier.

Some more options for the Lectin Free diet are:

- pasture-raised meats
- Brussels sprouts
- cooked sweet potatoes
- garlic
- leafy, green vegetables
- A2 milk
- celery
- avocado
- broccoli
- olives
- cruciferous vegetables
- EVOO

Least Inflammatory foods that contain little to no lectin

Oils can be a good resource for your diet. The main ones being caprylic acid, olive oil, and ghee. They are a great source of oil for cooking, as well.

- Beef
- Chicken
- Hemp protein
- Salmon
- Rice Protein
- Sardines
- Beef or chicken liver
- Pea protein
- Collagen
- Raw Honey (make sure it is clear, not cloudy)
- Glucose/dextrose
- Hi-Maize resistant starch
- Safflower oil
- Waxy Maize
- Bee Pollen
- Avocado oil
- Animal fat
- Caprylic Acid
- EVOO
- Ghee
- Hemp oil
- Romaine lettuce
- Grapeseed oil
- Carob
- Cucumbers
- Coconut oil
- Black Cumin seed oil
- Sunflower Lecithin
- Nutritional yeast
- Caffeine-free kombucha- not for histamine intolerant
- Steamed spinach
- Celery

- Cinnamon
- Steamed green beans
- Broccoli sprouts
- Brewer's yeast
- Pickles -not for histamine intolerant
- Steamed broccoli
- Mustard
- Steamed Kale
- Most spices
- Italian Seasoning
- Vanilla
- Trehalas
- Stevia
- Curry
- Xylitol
- Spirulina
- Vinegar, apple cider
- Leafy Greens
- Steamed collard greens
- Sauer kraut -not for histamine intolerant
- Mushrooms
- Decaf tea
- Sriracha

Foods that are not perfect but are good enough to eat

- Pomegranate
- Eggs- initially exclude these and only eat grass feed eggs, but if you have an egg allergy, then do not eat them at all.
- Anchovies
- Pork
- Beef gelatin
- Raw honey– cloudy
- Avocados
- Purple sweet potatoes
- Sugar snap peas

- Cantaloupe
- Honeydew
- Blueberries
- Cooked tempeh
- Green beans
- Tangerines
- Mango
- Garlic
- Onions
- Papaya -fresh
- Watermelon (seedless)
- Pineapple
- Snow peas
- Goldenberries

Foods that are okay

- Grapefruit
- Fully sprouted lentils or repeated soakings for over 48 hours
- Summer Squash
- Japanese sweet potatoes
- Blackberries
- Guava
- Chia seeds
- Coconut Milk
- Soaked/sprouted quinoa
- Oranges
- Sunflower seeds
- Sprouted sunflower seeds
- Flaxseed -preferably sprouted
- Coconut Shreds
- Sesame seeds
- Cranberries
- Kiwi
- Hemp seeds
- Dates

- Pears
- Peaches
- Nectarines
- Jasmine Tea- contains small amounts of caffeine
- Raspberries
- Beets
- Cherries
- Kale chips
- Apples
- Plums
- Kudzu

How can you reduce the amount of lectin in foods? What cooking methods will help? Which foods will this work with?

Our ancestors have found several ways to decrease the number of lectins in our foods. They lived within a time period where "survival of the fittest" was the only way to live. They found solutions to enjoy foods that were abundant with lectins. Below is a detailed description of how each one of the methods that they used, can decrease the percentage of lectins in your food.

Sprouting can eliminate the lectins

Allowing for your grains, beans, and seeds to sprout is one way to decrease the lectin in your foods. The longer you allow them to sprout, the more chances you have of decreasing the lectins in them. Essentially, deactivating the effect of the lectin. However, make sure you check for the correct types of foods. Alfalfa sprouts should not be further sprouted since it increases the lectin content. Lectins are located in the coats of the seeds and beans when it germinates the seeds coat is then metabolically changed which eliminates lectins.

Soaking before you cook your beans will cook out the lectins.

That long soak, rinse and boil sequence that many women have used to prepare the beans and grains before cooking actually has a purpose. This process reduces the lectins in the beans. If you have ever noticed that your grandmother does this, now you know why. To soak out the lectins in the legumes or beans, you should change your water after 6-8 hours and then let them soak overnight. It is best to drain or rinse the beans before cooking, as well. To further neutralize the lectins, you can also cook them with sodium bicarbonate, or baking soda.

Fermenting is another option

When you ferment your food, you are allowing beneficial bacteria to be digested Without fermenting those bacteria once digested can convert into harmful bacteria. Some of the healthiest populations have been known to stick with soy products such as:

- Tempeh
- Tamari
- Natto
- Miso
- Some vegetables
- Cabbage

There are several cultures that have a long history of fermentation to treat grains. Sourdough bread as well as beer, have been fermented from grains. However, with all the lectins in our food, not all of them are destroyed by the process of fermentation. There are some that remain, no matter how long of a fermentation process you use. Due to this, you may not reduce the negative effects that are felt by everyone, just a few select people.

Since our stomachs are not designed to tolerate grains and beans, due to the lectin. Some people will consume alternative diets, such as high fruits and vegetables, instead of grains and beans. There are several varieties of seaweed and mucilaginous vegetables that have a high binding ability. This makes it hard to digest them in the gut. Lectins are resistant to dry heat, which explains why using a legume flour, that is raw, in your baked goods, is not something that should be taken lightly. It needs to be done with lots of caution.

Cooking with your pressure cooker

A pressure cooker can help with lowering the amount of lectin in your foods. Using a pressure cooker is a great way to eat healthier, without worrying about Lectins. When you cook with tomatoes, potatoes, beans, and quinoa, place them in a pressure cooker. This helps to destroy the lectins in the food. It will not get rid of all the lectins, but it will lower them enough. This will not work in the same way with rye, barley, spelt, oats, and wheat, though.

Peeling and deseeding fruits and veggies

By peeling and deseeding your fruits and veggies, you will reduce the lectins in them. The most harmful part of a plant, when it comes to lectin, is the hull, the peel, or the rind. The seeds and the peels are where most of the lectins are hiding. A way to significantly cut back on your lectin intake is to eliminate that part of the plant.

Hulling brown rice or choosing white over brown.

Choose white rice over brown rice for grains is a great way to lower lectins in your diet. If you do choose to consume brown rice, then strip the hull from the rice, since that is where all the lectin is contained. The hull is the most dangerous section of the rice.

Some more helpful tips to make the best of the Lectin Free Diet

Proper sleep

Make sure you are getting the proper amount of sleep required. Most people need 8 hours of sleep. This will help them rejuvenate and refresh their bodies.

Mild exercise

You should also get some light exercise in every day. This can be something as simple as a brisk walk. As with any new change in your lifestyle, it will not be easy. If you work at it, then it will definitely be worth your while. Take it slowly and go at your own pace.

Eat a proper diet without lectins

Eat as many of the foods listed above that are yes foods, unless it is protein, then you should only eat 4 -oz. per day. When you start the cleanse, you can begin the process of changing your bad bacteria to good bacteria, in your gut. Maintain the lectin free diet after the cleanse, and you will be able to heal your gut.

Leave out the fruit in your smoothies

When making the smoothie from Phase 1, leave out the fruit. Instead of making a fruit smoothie, make a veggie smoothie. Green bananas and avocados are the exceptions to this rule. The reason being that these fruits are loaded with vitamins, fats, and fiber that is beneficial to your body's needs. They also do not have any sugar. Avocados are high in vitamins that support blood cell functions and nerve support. They are also loaded with fats, that will help you lower your cholesterol and protect against heart disease. Green bananas are abundant in fiber, vitamin B-6, and potassium, and contain no sugar.

Replace a few things in your pantry, with healthier options.

Slowly replacing your bad foods, with healthier options, is a step in the right direction. Replace your corn meal, white table sugar, and whole wheat flour with gut-friendly, healthier options so you can start to heal your gut.

Try dark chocolate instead of milk chocolate

With your daily allowance of chocolate, make sure the chocolate is dark chocolate. There is no sugar in dark chocolate. This helps to eliminate more sugar from your diet and still adds a great treat. If dark chocolate is not your favorite, then start by going through the variety of chocolate until you are able to eat dark chocolate easily. Once you get used to no sugar in your diet, dark chocolate will become your new favorite treat.

Make your own salad dressing to eliminate lectin

Salad dressing is more expensive when bought in the bottle. It is easier and healthier to make it at home. So, make your own. You can use 2 ingredients, olive oil, and vinegar to make an amazing vinaigrette. There are many flavors of vinegar on the market. You are guaranteed to find one you will like. If you want a creamy salad dressing, then consider adding chopped dill and other herbs to a sheep or goats milk yogurt. This can be a great addition to any meal. Another salad dressing that is healthy and decadent is avocado dressing. Experiment until you find the right dressing for you.

Try to eat only grass-fed ground beef

With modern farming techniques, farmers are using grain feeds to feed their cattle and chickens. This grain feed is loaded with lectins. By eating a diet of grass-fed cattle and chicken, you can reduce your intake of lectins. Plus, it tastes much better.

Make a meal in your pressure cooker

Pressure cookers are an easy way to make a meal, in one-pot, and reduce the lectins, while you are cooking it. A pressure cooker can be used for almost any recipe. Experimenting with pressure cookers is part of the fun of a lectin free diet.

Making your own tortillas will eliminate the lectin

Instead of using store-bought flour tortillas, try making your own and having some fun with your dinners. Start a new tradition with the family. Eating lectin free meals that are easy to prepare and involve teaching the kids how to cook.

Skip the Hummus and have tahini instead

Instead of eating hummus, which is not thoroughly cooked, which doesn't reduce all the lectin out, try tahini, for your dipping needs. Tahini is made with ground up sesame seeds. This is one of the key ingredients in hummus, which provides it with the famous flavor that is associated with hummus. It is also a good source of cholesterol-lowering fats. Sesame seeds have a strong flavor, and you will find that you need to use less. Tahini is a great addition to add to any salad or salad dressing, as well as soups for those cold days.

Skip a meal or two

Skipping a meal or two can be easy when you are busy. The next time you find that you are not hungry, then skip that meal. Just because society dictates when to eat, doesn't mean you have to follow that schedule. Stop scheduling meals down to the minute and letting the clock dictate when you have a meal. Your body may be on a totally different eating schedule, then you think.

Chapter 3: The phases of a Lectin Free Diet

When moving from a diet full of lectin to a diet without lectin, you will need to first prepare your body for the changes that are about to take place. You should also prepare your mind so that it can fully understand which foods good and which ones are not. To prepare your gut, you will need to take several steps to ensure that your body is getting the full benefit of the lectin free diet.
Within 3 days you will see benefits such as:

- Reduction in inflammation
- Improved gut bacteria balance
- Reduction in water weight and eventually actual weight due to excess food.
- An improved sense of well-being.

Phase 1

To prepare your already damaged gut, start with a cleanse. This cleanse below is based on a 3-day plant detox. This detox will kick-start the lectin diet and clean out your gut. This allows the bacteria in your gut to change to only allow the good bacteria into your gut. When you repel the bad gut bacteria, you start to feel less sick or fat.
The detox will also help you to stimulate an immune response.

Detox days

Start this detox by saying "NO!" to several foods, which are listed below.

- Grains or pseudo-grains
- Soy
- Dairy

- Soy
- Fruit
- Farm animal proteins
- Nightshade plants
- Veggies
- Sugar
- Seeds
- Eggs
- Inflammatory oils
- Canola
- Roots
- Tubers
- Corn

You will need to replace your meal choices with some new staple ingredients. These will be lectin free ingredients or ones that have had the lectin greatly reduced in them. These dishes should be consumed over the first three days of your phase 1 of the lectin free diet.

- Radicchio
- Chinese cabbage
- Cruciferous
- Swiss chard
- Cauliflower
- Broccoli
- Brussels sprouts
- Raw sauerkraut
- Bok choy
- Chives
- Napa cabbage
- Kimchi
- Cabbage
- Nepalis cactus
- Arugula
- Watercress
- Collards
- Kale
- Endive
- Carrots
- Mesclun
- Celery
- Artichokes
- Cilantro
- Daikon radishes
- Onions
- Leeks
- Scallions
- Chicory
- Radishes
- Butter lettuce
- Mustard greens Carrot greens
- Mizuna
- Beets
- Leafy greens

- Dandelion greens
- Algae
- Garlic
- Artichokes
- Escarole
- Spinach
- Hearts of palm
- Purslane
- Okra
- Asparagus
- Fennel
- Romaine
- Kohlrabi
- Seaweed
- Mushrooms
- Sea vegetables
- Perilla
- Parsley
- Basil
- Mint

The above vegetables are all powerhouse vegetables. This means that they provide a high nutrient-rich diet. The USDA says that dark leafy greens supply a good amount of folate. Folate is a good for your heart and bones, providing a large quantity of vitamin K, which can help prevent inflammatory issues. You can consume as much of the above vegetables as you would like. They can be cooked or raw when consumed. However, if you already suffer from a gut issue or irritable bowel syndrome, you may want to make sure your vegetables are thoroughly cooked. Fresh or frozen vegetables that are organic are best.

Protein

Small portions of fish and protein are a great option to eat while on the Phase 1 cleanse. While cleansing your gut, for the lectin free diet, consuming small portions of fish and pasture raised chicken is an acceptable option for protein. However, consuming more than 4-oz. of wild caught fish or pasture raised chicken in a day is not recommended. 4-oz. would be equivalent to a deck of cards.

Oils and good Fats

When it comes to fats and oils, there is a distinction between good and bad. One good fat would be an avocado. It is a good idea to eat as many avocados as you would like. Oils are good in moderation. Below is a list of oils that can be used without worrying if the lectin levels are too high.

- Hemp seed

- Coconut
- Macadamia nut
- Walnut
- Flaxseed
- EVOO
- Avocado
- Sesame seed

Dressing and sauces are another great option as well as seasonings.

Everyone loves a little dressing with their salad, but on a typical diet, the dressing adds calories. However, with the lectin free diet, you can use specific types of dressings to accompany your salads. Simply stay clear of all processed dressings and sauces. Using a fresh lemon squeeze and some olive oil can enhance any meal. Also consider trying one of the dressing, sauces or seasonings listed below:

- Fresh spices
- Vinegar
- Sea salt
- Mustard
- Fresh cracked black pepper
- Fresh herbs

For drinks, while doing the lectin free diet, you want to drink 8 cups of water every day. The water should be tap or sparkling. Alternatively, you can drink unsweetened tea and or decaf coffee.

One of the ways to start phase 1, is to drink the green smoothie for breakfast, lunch, or dinner.

The Green Smoothie

This is a salad in a smoothie recipe.

Ingredients:

(1 c) tap H2O
(1 c) of romaine lettuce-chopped
(.25 c) ice cubes
(3-6 drops) stevia extract
(1) mint sprig
(.5 c) baby spinach
(.5) avocado
(4 tablespoons) lemon juice

Preparation Method:

Blend all ingredients into your blender until smooth.

What do you do when you are having snack cravings?

We all have cravings and while on a cleanse you are definitely going to have cravings. What can you do while on the cleanse if the cravings get too intense? One of the best ways to fill that crunchy craving need and still eat healthy, with a low lectin level option, is to eat a lettuce boat with some guacamole. Or maybe a half avocado with some lemon juice drizzled on top. Add some olive oil, and you have yourself a delicious snack that will sustain you for a while. You can also try eating some healthy nut choices such as pistachio, chestnuts, pine nuts, macadamia nuts, pecans, hazelnuts, and walnuts. Olives are another great snack for munching when the cravings are just too much. Olives help jump-start the anti-inflammatory effects quickly.

Phase 2

<u>Phase 2 is based on repair and restore</u>. In this phase, you will be eating lectin free for 6 weeks or more. You will eat from the approved food list and start to maintain your lectin free diet. In the phase 2 plan, you will consume no more than 4 -oz. of animal proteins or animal byproducts per meal.

Phase 2 WEEK 1 Meal Plan

DAY 1

- BREAKFAST Green Smoothie
- SNACK G c raw nuts
- LUNCH Stir-Fried Shrimp with Bok choy
- SNACK Romaine Lettuce Boats Filled with hummus
- DINNER Creamy spinach Ravioli with basil pesto sauce

DAY 2:
- BREAKFAST "Green" Egg-Sausage Muffin*
- SNACK G c raw nuts
- LUNCH Two hard-boiled eggs, grass feed, topped with Basil Pesto
- SNACK Romaine Lettuce Boats Filled with hummus
- DINNER Spinach Pizza with a mushroom crust; mixed green salad with avocado vinaigrette dressing

DAY 3
- BREAKFAST Paradox Smoothie
- SNACK G c raw nuts
- LUNCH Pastured chicken breast and cabbage slaw wrapped in lettuce leaves with sliced avocado*
- SNACK Romaine Lettuce Boats Filled with Guacamole
- DINNER Mashed parsnips with Fettucine Alfredo and fresh spring vegetables.

DAY 4
- BREAKFAST Cinnamon-Flaxseed Muffin in a Mug*
- SNACK G c raw nuts 15
- LUNCH Miracle Noodles or other konjac noodles tossed with olive oil, salt, and pepper; Boston lettuce salad with vinaigrette
- SNACK Romaine Lettuce Boats Filled with Guacamole
- DINNER Grilled Portabella-Pesto Mini "Pizzas"; a salad of your choice with vinaigrette; steamed artichoke

DAY 5

- BREAKFAST Green Smoothie
- SNACK G c raw nuts
- LUNCH "Raw" Mushroom Soup; a salad of your choice with vinaigrette
- SNACK Brussel sprout chips with Arugula thyme pesto
- DINNER Creamy spinach Ravioli with basil pesto sauce

DAY 6

- BREAKFAST Perfect Plantain Pancakes*
- SNACK G c raw nuts
- LUNCH creamy soup with Brussel sprouts chips and arugula pesto
- SNACK Romaine Lettuce Boats Filled with Guacamole
- DINNER Creamy spinach Ravioli with basil pesto sauce oven fries

DAY 7

- BREAKFAST Green Smoothie
- SNACK G c raw nuts
- LUNCH Prosciutto, sweet potatoes, and arugula salad
- SNACK Brussel sprout chips with Arugula thyme pesto
- DINNER Grilled Portabella-Pesto Mini "Pizzas"; orange and salmon salad

Phase 2 WEEK 2 Meal Plan

DAY 1
- BREAKFAST Coconut-Almond Flour Muffin in a Mug*
- SNACK G c raw nuts
- LUNCH Grilled pastured chicken breast*; Shaved Kohlrabi with Crispy Pear and Nuts
- SNACK Brussel sprout chips with Arugula thyme pesto
- DINNER Marinated Grilled Cauliflower steaks with orange and salmon salad and lemon oil vinaigrette

DAY 2
- BREAKFAST Green Smoothie
- SNACK G c raw nuts
- LUNCH Stir-fry shrimp and bok choy salad with vinaigrette
- SNACK Romaine Lettuce Boats Filled with Guacamole
- DINNER Grilled Alaska salmon with Roasted romaine and cob salad with oven fries

DAY 3
- BREAKFAST avocado toast with egg spinach and goat cheese omelet
- SNACK G c raw nuts
- LUNCH 3 Roasted lemon pepper cabbage wedges with oven fries
- SNACK Romaine Lettuce Boats Filled with mashed parsnips

- DINNER Grilled portobello mushroom pizza minis with salmon and arugula pesto

DAY 4

- BREAKFAST Green Smoothie
- SNACK G c raw nuts
- LUNCH Canned sardines in olive oil mashed with H avocado and splash of balsamic vinegar, and wrapped in lettuce leaves*
- SNACK Brussel sprout chips with Arugula thyme pesto
- DINNER Marinated Grilled Cauliflower steaks with orange and salmon salad and lemon oil vinaigrette

DAY 5

- BREAKFAST Ginger cake with cinnamon in a mug
- SNACK G c raw nuts
- LUNCH Creamy soup with vanilla cake in a mug
- SNACK Romaine Lettuce Boats Filled with Guacamole
- DINNER Cranberry apple chicken with cabbage and shrimp and escarole salad

DAY 6

- BREAKFAST Green Smoothie
- SNACK G c raw nuts
- LUNCH Prosciutto, sweet potatoes, and arugula salad
- SNACK Romaine Lettuce Boats Filled with Guacamole
- DINNER Sorghum Salad with Radicchio topped with Alaska salmon*

DAY 7

- BREAKFAST Cassava Flour Waffles with a Collagen Kick*
- SNACK G c raw nuts
- LUNCH Arugula salad topped with a small can of tuna* with perilla oil and vinegar dressing
- SNACK Brussel sprout chips with Arugula thyme pesto
- DINNER Veggie Curry with Sweet Potato "Noodles"; Baked Okra Lectin-Blocking Chips

Phase 3

This is a 5-day modified vegan fast that helps you reap the rewards. You will continue to eat similar to the Phase 2 plan only you will reduce your proteins that come from animal products or meat. This should be reduced down to 2-oz. per meal, instead of the 4-oz. per meal in phase 2. This means you should only have 4-oz. per day of protein-based meat or meat by-product.

Phase 3 Meal Plan

DAY 1
- BREAKFAST Green Smoothie
- SNACK Romaine Lettuce Boats Filled with Guacamole
- LUNCH Prosciutto, sweet potatoes, and arugula salad
- SNACK Brussel sprout chips with Arugula thyme pesto
- DINNER Vegan version of Cabbage-Kale Sauté with Salmon and Avocado, using grain-free tempeh

DAY 2
- BREAKFAST Green Smoothie
- SNACK Romaine Lettuce Boats Filled with Guacamole
- LUNCH Vegan version of Romaine Salad with Avocado and Cilantro-Pesto Chicken, using grain-free tempeh 19
- SNACK Romaine Lettuce Boats Filled with Guacamole
- DINNER Lemony Brussels Sprouts, Kale, and Onions with Cabbage "Steak"

DAY 3
- BREAKFAST Green Smoothie
- SNACK Romaine Lettuce Boats Filled with Guacamole

- LUNCH Vegan version of Chicken-Arugula-Avocado Seaweed Wrap with Cilantro Dipping Sauce, using hemp tofu
- SNACK Brussel sprout chips with Arugula thyme pesto
- DINNER Roasted Broccoli with Cauliflower "Rice" and Sautéed Onions

DAY 4

- BREAKFAST Green Smoothie
- SNACK Romaine Lettuce Boats Filled with Guacamole
- LUNCH Prosciutto, sweet potatoes, and arugula salad
- SNACK Romaine Lettuce Boats Filled with hummus
- DINNER Lemony Brussels Sprouts, Kale, and Onions with Cabbage "Steak

DAY 5

- BREAKFAST Green Smoothie
- SNACK Romaine Lettuce Boats Filled with Guacamole
- LUNCH Prosciutto, sweet potatoes, and arugula salad
- SNACK Romaine Lettuce Boats Filled with egg spinach and cheese omelet
- DINNER Roasted lemon pepper cabbage wedges with oven fries

Phases goal and time

Each phases goal and the length of time that you should be on this phase:

Phase 1' goal is to cleanse your gut of bad bacteria and start producing good bacteria. This will help with healing the gut and start your body on a lectin free diet. The Phase 1 cycle should last about 3 days. It is a way to kick-start your body into being prepared to eat a lectin free diet.

Phase 2's goal is to repair the gut and restore the gut. In phase 1 we are preparing the gut for phase 2. You can do phase 2 without phase 1, but you cannot do phase 1 without phase 2. Phase 2 should last a minimum of 6 weeks. You can create meal plans for phase 2 out of the acceptable foods, or you can use a sample meal plan and alternate how you eat for the next 6 weeks or more.

Phase 3 is all about reaping the rewards. When you get to phase 3, your process is to reap the rewards of phase 1 and 2 and decrease your meat intake down even more. This helps you to see bigger changes in your health. Phase 3 is the 5-day modified vegan fast, and within this time period, you reduce your intake of specific nutrients, after the 5 days you return to phase 2.

Phase 1 Cycle

Phase 1 can start like this:

DAY 1
- BREAKFAST Green Smoothie
- SNACK Romaine Lettuce Boats Filled with Guacamole
- LUNCH Arugula Salad with Chicken and Lemon Vinaigrette*
- SNACK Romaine Lettuce Boats Filled with Guacamole
- DINNER Cabbage-Kale Sauté with Salmon and Avocado*

DAY 2
- BREAKFAST Green Smoothie
- SNACK Romaine Lettuce Boats Filled with Guacamole
- LUNCH Romaine Salad with Avocado and Cilantro-Pesto Chicken*
- SNACK Romaine Lettuce Boats Filled with Guacamole
- DINNER Lemony Brussels Sprouts, Kale, and Onions with Cabbage "Steak"

DAY 3
- BREAKFAST Green Smoothie
- SNACK Romaine Lettuce Boats Filled with Guacamole

- LUNCH Chicken-Arugula-Avocado Seaweed Wrap with Cilantro Dipping Sauce*
- SNACK Romaine Lettuce Boats Filled with Guacamole
- DINNER Roasted Broccoli with Cauliflower "Rice" and Sautéed Onions

When cooking a lectin free diet, you need to adjust your grocery budget. Instead of focusing on your spending, focus more on how and when you spend. Try dividing your list into 3 parts. Each part is designated for a specific need. Such as your weekly list, your monthly list, and your seasonal list.

Weekly list

This list will be used the most throughout your lectin free dieting. This is the items you purchase most frequently. These would be a fridge, freezer, and pantry items. Sometimes this is the only list that people will use. Most people will make a list of the grocery items they need for that weeks' worth of meals. This is the same thing, only it is designed to help you eat the lectin free diet. As you go through and make these lists, you will find that you may be overlapping on ingredients.

Monthly list

This list you should make at the beginning of the month, and it should contain non-perishables for the pantry. By this time these items will be getting low.

- French or Italian butter
- Olive oil
- Frozen vegetables
- Nuts

- Hot sauce
- Unsweetened coconut milk
- Birch Benders Paleo pancake mix
- Vinegar
- Stevia
- Dried herbs/seasonings
- Almond flour

Seasonal list

This one should be the one you enjoy most. When every season starts, you should sit down and list the items that you need to buy, in bulk and freeze. Freezing them helps you to have several months' worth of food. This would be your meat and fish shopping trip. You should be able to save money since you will be buying in bulk. You will also find, that you are saving money, by living a lectin free diet, since your health will improve, your medical costs will reduce, and your doctor bills will be less.

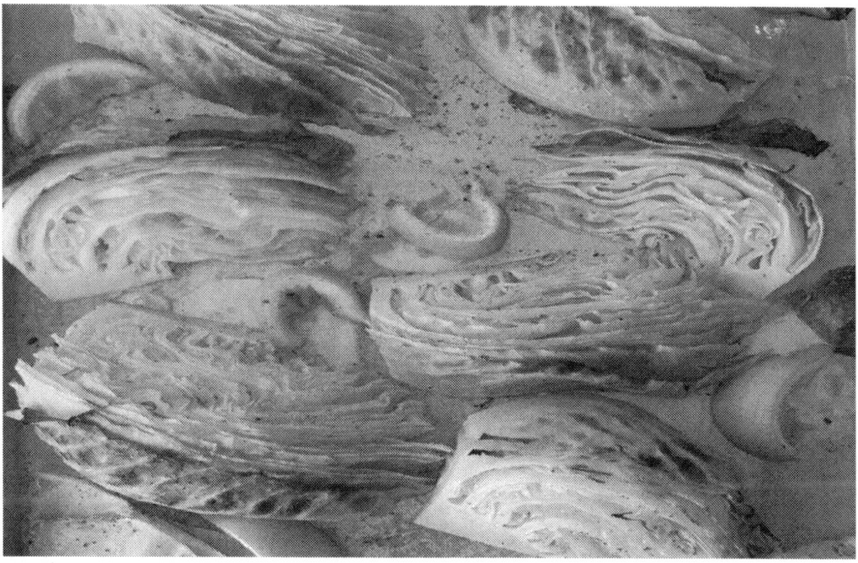

Chapter 4: Recipes For The Lectin Free Diet Traditionally Cooked

Meats and meat-based dishes

Egg, Spinach, and Goat Cheese Breakfast
Yields: 4 single servings
Phase: 1-2-3
Cook & Prep: 15 Min

Ingredients:
EVOO (2 tablespoons)
Himalayan sea salt Pinch
black pepper Pinch
spinach-chopped (2 oz.)
cloves of garlic thinly sliced (2)
eggs, beaten (6)
goat cheese crumbled (4 oz.)
6-8-inch cassava flour tortilla (8), handmade tortillas

Preparation Method:

1. Using your skillet, heated to medium temp., pour in your cooking oil. Once you have heated your oil add in the ingredients: spinach, salt, garlic, and pepper.

2. Begin to cook the spinach until it becomes wilted. At this time, the spinach should be completely cooked. This will take you about 2-3 min. Make sure you spread the spinach out across the skillet so that it cooks evenly. This should only take you 2-3 min.

3. Next, pour your scrambled eggs over the spinach/garlic mix in the skillet, letting them cook for 30 seconds. Then, proceed to stir the eggs around the pan, with your spatula until they completely set. This should be another 3 to 4 min. of cooking time.

4. Turn off the stove, removing the skillet from the heat. Then, proceed to spread your goat cheese over the top of your egg mixture. Allowing the egg mix to sit while the cheese softens.

5. While you are waiting, heat your premade tortillas on a microwave-safe plate, using a damp towel covering the tortillas, to retain moisture. Heating just 4 tortillas at a time, each set should be heated for about 30 seconds.

6. Now, spoon some of your egg mixture into the center of each tortilla. Folding your stuffed tortilla like a taco, serve with salsa or guacamole.

Omelets and salad

Yields: 1 single serving
Phase: 1-2-3
Cook & Prep: 25 min

Ingredients:
Balsamic vinaigrette (.25 c)
Omega-3 eggs (2)
Arugula (.5 c)
Sea salt (1 teaspoon)
EVOO (.25 c)

Preparation Method:

1. Scramble your eggs in a coffee cup and then pour them into your pan which has been heated to a temperature of medium heat.
2. Let the bottom of the eggs cook until completely done. Right before the top is fully cooked, fold over the eggs to form a taco.
3. Continue to cook until the insides of the eggs are done. There should be no mushiness to the eggs.
4. Place the EVOO, Balsamic Vinegar, along with sea salt into a glass bowl and mix them until fully blended.
5. Using a plate, lay all your arugula out and top it with your cooked eggs.
6. Pour some dressing on top.
7. Serve and enjoy!

Chicken & Goat Cheese Enchiladas

Yields: 8 single servings
Phase: 2-3
Cook & Prep: 45 min

Ingredients:
EVOO (2 tablespoons)
shiitake mushrooms (8-oz.)
garlic cloves (4) peeled
white onion (1) chopped
ground cumin (.5 teaspoon)
goat cheese (8-oz.) crumbled
cooked pastured chicken (8-oz.) shredded
broths (2 c) divided
Vinegar, apple cider (3 teaspoons)
sea salt
cassava flour tortillas (8) warmed
oregano (.5 teaspoon) dry
black pepper
coconut aminos (1 teaspoon)

paprika (.25 teaspoon)
granular sweetener (1 teaspoon)
cilantro freshly chopped
hot sauce

Preparation Method:

1. Your oven should be pre-heated to a temperature of 400 degrees Fahrenheit.

2. Using a frying pan, pour in some oil, and warm it to medium/high heat. Throw in some mushrooms, along with onions, and continue to cook while stirring often. The onions and mushrooms should begin to soften as they cook. This will be approximately 6 or 8 minutes.

3. Next, add in the broth, chicken, salt, and pepper to the pot. Lower your heat to medium and cook for a bit longer, while continuing to stir. Most of the liquid should be adsorbed while you cook the chicken. When the liquid is absorbed completely, which only takes 4 minutes, you should move on to the next step. Transfer all your ingredients to a separate bowl while stirring in the goat cheese, about half will do.

4. While you wait, make the adobo sauce. Start by blending the left-over broth, cider vinegar, garlic, coconut aminos, sea salt, cumin, sweetener, oregano, and paprika in a mixer. Pushing the pulse button on the mixer, blend the ingredients until they are smooth. This should only take approximately 3 min.

5. Pour the adobo into a 9x13 in. glass dish for baking. Using a .25 measuring cup, scoop the mushroom mix into the tortillas. Roll your tortilla and lay them in the pan, with

their seams facing down. Once all the tortillas are in the pan, side by side, pour the left-over amount of adobo evenly across the tortilla tops.

6. Next, sprinkle the tops with the left-over goat cheese.

7. Bake the tortillas, until the sauce is bubbling, the goat cheese should be melted as well. This should take approximately 15 minutes. Use the hot sauce and cilantro to season the tacos.

*Recipe Notes: Preparing the chicken and tortillas beforehand allows this meal to only take 45 minutes the day of the meal, however, if the chicken and tortillas are not prepared, in advance, add in 1 hour to the total cook time.

Seafood, Salads, and vegetables

Roasted Lemon Pepper Cabbage Wedges.

Yields: 6 single servings
Phase: 2-3
Cook & Prep: 30 min

Ingredients:
Lemon-wedges (1)
cabbage-wedge (1) medium head
fresh ground pepper
Avocado oil (.5 Tablespoon)

Alternatives:

- Coconut oil
- EVOO

sea salt (pinch)

Preparation Method:

1. Start with preheating the oven to a temperature of 450 degrees Fahrenheit.

2. Brushing the outside edges of your cabbage lightly, with oil, to ensure they do not burn. Making sure to evenly coat each piece of cabbage.

3. Next, lay the cabbage carefully on a baking sheet. Leave space in between each wedge, allowing them to be able to get crispy.

4. Using your seasonings, flavor the cabbage to your liking.

5. Roast your cabbage wedges for roughly 15 minutes. Once done, flip the wedges over and roast another 10 minutes, or so. Continue to cook them so that the outer edges are crispy, & the center is tender.

6. Garnish with a fresh wedge of Lemon.

Low Carb Crispy Seasoned Jicama Fries

Yield: 4 single servings
Phase: 1-2-3
Cook & Prep: 1 h 10 min

Ingredients:
salt, for taste (1-2 teaspoon)
jicama (1-lb)
butter or oil (3 tbs)
onion (.5 teaspoon) powdered
black pepper a dash
garlic (.5 teaspoon) powdered
chili (1 teaspoon) powdered
paprika a dash

Preparation Method:

1. Heat your oven to a temperature of 400 degrees Fahrenheit.

2. Laying the jicama on a cutting board, proceed to peel and then slice the jicama into shapes similar to a French fry.

3. In a pot, with salted water, bring your jicama to boiling. They should boil for 15 minutes, or until softened. Next,

take them out of the pot, allowing them to dry by patting with a towel or paper.

4. Next, allow the butter to melt, blending it with the oil, and all of the seasonings.

5. Toss the jicama into the seasoning mix, making sure to evenly coat them.

6. Spread the jicama sticks in a single layer, with none touching each other, and place them in the oven on the center rack of the oven. Proceed to bake for 40 mins. Remember to flip them halfway through to ensure even coating.

7. Once they are done, remove the jicama from your oven. Let the jicama rest for 3-4 minutes. Serve with some of your favorite dip.

*Note: If the crispiness is not to your liking, then cook them another 3-4 min, to make sure they are crispy enough.

Mashed Cauliflower

Yields: 4 single servings
Phase: 1-2-3
Cook & Prep: 20 min

Ingredients:
Chopped Chives and rosemary
shredded real Italian cheese (pecorino, Romano or Parmigiano-Reggiano) (.5 cs)
cauliflower florets –steamed (2 lbs.)
French or Italian butter (2 tablespoons)

Preparation Method:

1. Steam your cauliflower until it is softened.
2. Using a potato masher, mash the cauliflower adding in butter for creaminess.
3. Once mashed, add in the Italian cheeses and your seasonings. Blend it all together and serve.

Mashed Sweet Potatoes

Yields: 4 single servings
Phase: 1-2-3
Cook & Prep: 20 min

Ingredients:
cinnamon (.5 teaspoon)
sweet potatoes (2 lbs.) steamed, peeled, & diced
Scallions
Pecans finely chopped
pinch of allspice
almond milk (.25 c)
French or Italian butter (4 tablespoons)
salt (1 teaspoon)

Preparation Method:

1. Start by peeling, dicing, and steaming your sweet potatoes.

2. Once they have softened use a potato masher, almond milk, and butter to mash the potatoes to a creamy consistency.

3. Add in salt, allspice, and cinnamon, for flavor. Continuing to blend it all together.

4. Top the sweet potato mash with some scallions and chopped pecans.

5. Serve and enjoy!

Mashed Parsnips

Yields: 4 single servings
Phase: 1-2-3
Cook & Prep: 20 min

Ingredients:
A variety of chopped, fresh herbs:

- mint
- thyme
- sage
- rosemary

parsnips-diced, peeled and steamed (2 lbs.)
pepper, black (.25 teaspoon)
coriander (.5 teaspoon)
salt (.5 teaspoon)
coconut milk (.25 c)
French or Italian butter (4 tablespoons)
cloves minced garlic (2)

Preparation Method:

1. Start by peeling, dicing, and steaming, 2 lbs. of parsnips.

2. Once steamed, place them in the mixing bowl and mix in coconut milk, and butter.

3. Using a potato masher, mash them until they are creamy. Then, add in the garlic, salt, pepper, and coriander.

4. Blend it all together, topping it with chopped herbs such as mint, thyme, sage or rosemary.

Prosciutto, Sweet Potato, and Arugula Salad

Yields: 4 single servings
Phase: 2
Cook & Prep: 20 minutes

Ingredients:
fresh tarragon leaves (.25 c)
sea salt
EVOO (.25 c)
sweet potato- peeled, cubed (1-lb.)
black pepper
prosciutto di Parma-shredded (2-oz.)
imported Swiss cheese-shredded(2-oz.)
vinegar, white wine (1 tablespoon)
baby arugula(5-oz.)
Dijon mustard (1 tablespoon)
Parmigiano-Reggiano-shaved (.25 c)

Preparation Method:

1. Place your sweet potatoes in your boiler. Using cold water, cover them all the way, ensuring that they are completely covered by water. Allow them to boil until they are softened.

2. Add some salt to the pot and lower the temperature of the eye. Continue to allow them to simmer until done. When they are ready, they will be tender. This will take approximately 12 minutes. Once done drain them. After draining the pot place the potatoes under cool water to cool them off. Next, using a cutting board and knife, dice the potatoes into smaller pieces.

3. While waiting, use your whisk, and blend your vinegar, oil, mustard, and pepper to the desired consistency, that you like. Add salt to the potatoes to flavor for your preferred flavor.

4. Divide your arugula between 4 bowls. Top your arugula with Swiss cheese, prosciutto, sweet potatoes, and tarragon. Drizzle with your favorite dressing and flavor with parmigiana.

Grilled Portobello Pesto Pizza Minis.

Yields: 2 single servings
Phase: 2-3
Cook & Prep: 35 min

Ingredients:
portobello mushrooms (2) large
EVOO or Coconut
ball buffalo mozzarella (cut .25 or .5-inch slices) (1)
Sea salt, preferably iodized
basil pesto (6 tablespoons)
slices Italian prosciutto (2)
black pepper-cracked

Preparation Method:

1. Turn on your oven and heat it to a temperature of 325 degrees Fahrenheit. Lay the Mushroom caps, bottoms down, on the sheet pan. Using olive oil, rub them to prevent them from burning. Set your timer for 5 min and bake until they are slightly brown and crispy. Flip them over and bake another 5 minutes. Making sure each side is slightly brown and crispy.

2. Scoop your pesto on to the mushroom caps, about 3 tablespoons will do, add the prosciutto, in 1 slice increments. Make sure the prosciutto fits nicely inside the cap.

3. Then, using the mozzarella slices, lay the cheese on top of the caps. Repeat this process with each mushroom cap.

4. Re-insert the pan, with the mushroom caps, into the oven for 5 minutes more. The cheese should be gooey when done.

5. Season with some salt and pepper, or your favorite seasoning.

6. Serve and enjoy!

Baked Sweet Potato with Garlic and Kale

Yields: 2 single servings
Phase: 1-2-3
Cook & Prep: 20 min

Ingredients:
sweet potato(6-oz.)
Olive oil (.25 teaspoon)
Kale (.5 c)
Garlic (.25 teaspoon)
Salt

Preparation Method:

1. Heat your oven to a temperature of 350 degrees Fahrenheit.

2. Place your sweet potato into a piece of tin foil and pierce the potato with a fork, in several locations, for venting. Roll the foil around the potato, creating a jacket. Then place the foil-wrapped potato on a sheet pan. Do this with every single potato.

3. Set your timer for 30 minutes and place them in the oven to bake. Check and ensure that the potatoes are soft all the way through before removing them from the oven.

4. When the potatoes are done, remove them from the foil and place your potatoes into a bowl for mashing. Using the potato masher, proceed to mash the potatoes and add some kale, olive oil, garlic, and salt for garnish and flavor.

5. Top with cheese, if you like.

6. Enjoy.

Stir Fried Shrimp with Bok Choy

Yields: 4 single servings
Phase: 2-3
Cook & Prep: 10 min

Ingredients:
Large bag of Wild shrimp
Sesame oil (.25 teaspoon)
Ginger (.25 teaspoon)
Garlic (.5 teaspoon)
Bok choy (.75 c)

Preparation Method:

1. Using a wok, stir-fry the shrimp, sesame oil, ginger, garlic, and Bok choy altogether. Blending all the flavors together. Continue to cook for 10 min. then serve with your favorite sauce.

Steak & Spinach Salad

Yields: 4 single servings
Phase: 1-2-3
Cook & Prep: 25 min

Ingredients:
pine nuts-toasted (2 tablespoons)
grass-fed steak-cooked, sliced (1 pound)
baby spinach (5-oz.)
shirataki rice (drained & rinsed) (1 c)

Yogurt Dressing
pepper
whole goat/sheep milk yogurt (1 c)
fresh thyme leaves (2 teaspoons)
salt
vinegar red wine (2 tablespoons)

Preparation Method:

1. In a skillet, on medium heat, cook your steak to medium rare.

2. This should be approximately 4 minutes, per side.

3. While cooking the steak, prepare the dressing. In a bowl, mix in the vinegar-red wine, whole goat/sheep milk yogurt, thyme leaves, salt and pepper with a whisk. Mix until all ingredients are well blended.

4. Prepare your rice as the package instructs you to.

5. Place your Spinach in a separate bowl and top with the rice, toasted pine nuts, steak, that has been sliced, and drizzle with your dressing.

6. Serve and enjoy!

Roasted Romain & Cobb Chicken Salad

Yields: 4 single servings
Phase: 1-2-3
Cook & Prep: 35 min

Ingredients:
Chicken-cooked, diced
goat cheese- crumbled(4-oz.)
roasted romaine hearts-chopped
bunch scallions-chopped (1)
hard-boiled eggs-sliced (2)
large, ripe avocados-sliced (2)

Adobo Cream Dressing
salt (1 teaspoon)
cumin (1 teaspoon)
heavy cream (.25 c)
lime juiced (1)
sour cream (.5 c)
adobo sauce from canned chipotles (1 tablespoon)

vinegar-red wine (1 tablespoon)

Preparation Method:

1. Pre-heat the temperature of your oven to 450 degrees Fahrenheit.

2. Using olive oil, brush 2 pastured chicken breast halves, (boneless, skinless) and 3 large hearts of romaine, (halved lengthwise) to prevent them from burning.

3. Using chili powder, cumin, salt, and pepper season the meat.

4. Bake chicken, on your baking sheet, that is lined with parchment, for around 10 minutes.

5. Arrange the romaine, with the cut side down, around the chicken on the pan. Bake for 10 minutes more. Ensuring that the lettuce is wilted and a little browned, around the edges. The chicken should be cooked all the way through, with no pink inside.

6. Next, using a whisk, blend all your ingredients for the dressing in your bowl.

7. While cooking the chicken breast, boil 2 of the eggs, until they are hard boiled.

8. Place your romaine and chicken, on your plate.

9. Garnish with avocado, cheese, and scallions on top, with egg crumbles.

10. Drizzle with your favorite dressing.

11. Serve and enjoy!

Meatballs & Bok Choy salad

Yields: 6 single serving
Phase: 1-2-3
Cook & Prep: 45 min

Ingredients:
heads baby bok choy-chopped (6)
cooked meatballs
scallions-thinly sliced (4)
chopped salted macadamia nuts (.25 c)
sautéed shiitake mushrooms (.5 c)
fresh cilantro-chopped (.5 c)

Red Pepper Vinaigrette:
coconut aminos (1 tablespoon)
lime juiced (3 tablespoons)
red pepper (.5 teaspoon)
golden monk fruit for sweetness (2 teaspoons)
sesame oil (1 tablespoon)

Preparation Method:

1. Mix the ground pork with the garlic that has been previously chopped. Add in a liberal sprinkling of salt, and pepper, if you like.

2. Form the mixture into 20, 1-inch meatballs. In an oiled pan, that is heated to a temperature of medium/high, cook the meatballs, making sure to turn often, so they do not brown. The meatballs should be fully cooked in approximately 8-10 minutes.

3. Remove the meatballs and place them on a plate, leaving the pan drippings in the pan for later use. Using a skillet, add in some shiitake mushrooms and proceed to sauté them for approximately 5 minutes.

4. Next, toss all the dressing ingredients together, in a separate bowl.

5. Then, toss the salad ingredients together, in another bowl.

6. On a plate, layer the meatballs with salad and pour the dressing on top.

7. Enjoy!

Orange & Salmon Salad

Yields: 4 single servings
Phase: 1-2-3
Cook & Prep: 30 min

Ingredients:
toasted hazelnuts-chopped (.333 c)
real Feta cheese-crumbled(2-oz)
baby spinach(5-oz.)
broiled or canned wild salmon-flaked(1-lb.)
red onion – thinly sliced (1) small
Navel oranges sectioned-peeled (2)

Dijon Vinaigrette
lemon juiced (1)
Dijon mustard (1 teaspoon)
fresh dill-chopped (1 tablespoon)
salt
honey (optional) (1 teaspoon)
vinegar white wine (3 tablespoons)
EVOO (4 tablespoons)

Preparation Method:

1. Mix your baby spinach with the red onions, navel orange pieces, and salmon flakes.

2. Pour the hazelnut and feta cheese on top and tossing it, to mix it all together.

3. Next, using a bowl, make your dressing by mix all ingredients together. Then drizzle the dressing over the salad.

4. Serve and enjoy!

Kale and Serrano Ham Salad

Yields: 4 single servings
Phase: 1-2-3
Cook & Prep: 30 min

Ingredients:
pine nuts (.25 c)
sweet onion sliced thinly (1)
Grated Parmesan cheese (2-oz.)
bunch kale, torn (1)
serrano ham diced(2-oz.)

Lemon oil
tablespoon olive oil (2)
salt to taste
lemon juiced (.5)

Tahini Sauce
lemon juiced (1)
tahini (stirred) (2 tablespoon)
EVOO (1 tablespoon)
white miso (2 tablespoons)
honey (2 teaspoons)

Preparation Method:

1. Start by preparing your Lemon oil. In a bowl, pour lemon juice, salt, and EVOO and begin to whisk them together, until they are fully blended.

2. Next, in a separate bowl, prepare the Tahini sauce. Start, by pouring white miso, honey, lemon juice, EVOO, and tahini into a separate bowl. Then proceed to whisk the ingredients until fully blended.

3. Now, place the Kale, and onions that have been diced, along with cheese, and pine nuts into a bowl, proceed to toss it all together to mix thoroughly. Drizzle your lemon oil, along with the tahini sauce, on top and toss again to blend well.

4. Place the salad onto 4 separate plates and serve.

Shrimp and Escarole Salad

Yields: 4 single servings
Phase: 1-2-3
Cook & Prep time: 15 min

Ingredients:
red onion-sliced (.5)
cooked shrimp (tail-on) (1-lb.)
head escarole, leaves-torn (1)
bunch radishes-quartered (1)

Caper-herb dressing
pepper
Dijon mustard (1 teaspoon)
Shallot-finely chopped (1) small
chives-fresh chopped (2 tablespoons)
vinegar white wine (2 tablespoons)
capers (2 tablespoons)
EVOO (.25 c)
garlic minced (2 cloves) (1 teaspoon)
salt

Preparation Method:

1. Start with mixing the Caper-herb vinaigrette in a bowl. Begin by placing all the ingredients into the bowl and proceed to whisk until fully blended.

2. Next place the cooked shrimp, escarole, onions, and radishes into a separate bowl and drizzle the vinaigrette on top. Toss it all together and serve on four separate plates.

Oven Fries

Yields: 8 single servings
Phase: 2
Cook & Prep: 40 minutes

Ingredients:
purple carrots – peeled, halved, and quartered lengthwise (4)
grainy mustard (3 tablespoons)
granulated garlic (2 teaspoons)
sweet potatoes-peeled, cut into .25-in. strips (2) medium
yuca roots-peeled, cut into .25-in strips (2) medium
sour cream (.75 c) full fat
EVOO (3 tablespoons)
sea salt (2 teaspoons)
black pepper

Preparation Method:

1. Place two baking sheets in the oven. One on the top rack and the other on the third rack. Proceed to heat your oven to a temperature of 450 degrees Fahrenheit.

2. In a bowl, mix the sweet potatoes, yuca, and carrots with EVOO. Then mix in black pepper, garlic-granulated, and salt, tossing for an even coating. Divide the ingredients between the two preheated baking sheets.

3. Bake until the ingredients are golden and crispy. Rotate the baking sheets from top to bottom when halfway done, by tossing the fries.

4. While you wait for them to cook, proceed to the next step. In another bowl mix the sour cream, mustard, and seasonings, to create the dip.

5. When the fries are done transfer them to a plate and serve with the prepared mustard dip.

Pasta and rice

Brown Butter Basil Sauce with Sweet potato Gnocchi

Yields: 4 single servings
Phase: 2-3
Cook & Prep: 1 h

Ingredients:
Gnocchi
cassava flour (.5 c)
sea salt (.5 teaspoon)
sweet potato-peeled, cut into 4-5 chunks (1) (1-pound)
large egg omega-3 or pastured (1)

Sauce
fresh basil-torn and divided (.5 c)
butter French or Italian-unsalted (3 tablespoons)
black pepper (1 teaspoon)
clove garlic-crushed (1)
small lemon-zested and juiced (.5)
Parmigiana-Reggiano-grated (.25 c)
sea salt (1 teaspoon)

Preparation Method:

1. Start by making the gnocchi. Cover the gnocchi with some water, ensuring that they are fully covered. Allow them to boil, and then lower your temperature to allow them to simmer. The pot should be partially covered, with a lid. Continue to cook for approximately 15 minutes. Drain the sweet potatoes and let them cool.

2. Next, mash them with a potato masher in a bowl.

3. Now, add in your eggs, with a pinch of salt. Using your hands, knead the mix, while adding in the flour. You should be making the dough at this time. Make sure to add enough flour so the dough will not stick to your fingers, but you do not want it crumbly.

4. Boil your pot of water, with a pinch of salt.

5. While you wait for the water to boil, roll the chunks of dough into some long, thin snakes. They should be the width of your thumb. Next, cut each snake into inch long pieces. Now, using your hand to grip, use your other thumb to place a shallow indent in each piece.

6. Drop your gnocchi pieces into your boiling water using a spoon with slits in it. When the gnocchi is floating, to the surface, start to remove them with the spoon and place in a covered dish to keep warm. Work in batches of 2 or more.

7. Place some butter in a skillet and prepare your sauce, by melting it over medium heat.

8. Then, using a skillet, sauté some garlic, while stirring continuously. Cook the butter for 4 min. until it browns.

9. Now, place your basil and gnocchi into the skillet. While cooking, mix the ingredients together by tossing. Cook until the gnocchi are lightly browned, and the basil should be wilted, this takes approximately 2 min.

10. Finally, stir lemon zest, salt, lemon juice, and pepper in a bowl. Serve with a garnish of basil and cheese.

Miracle Noodles with Pesto & Broccoli

Yields: 4 single servings
Phase: 2-3
Cook &Prep time: 20 min

Ingredients:
Miracle Noodles (1) bag
Basil pesto (½ c)
Olive oil (¼ teaspoon)
Broccoli florets (1 c)

Preparation Method:

1. Cook your miracle noodles by following the directions on the package.

2. Using a pan, add in the noodles, pesto, broccoli florets, and olive oil. Cook for approximately 10 minutes. Until the broccoli is softened. Season with whatever your favorite seasoning is. Mix it all together, making sure it is well blended.

3. When it is done, place it in a bowl and enjoy.

Creamy Spinach Ravioli with Basil Pesto

Yields: 1 single serving
Phase: 2-3
Cook & Prep: 35 minutes

Ingredients:
Spinach-squeezed dry, chopped, thawed (1 10-oz) package
EVOO-divided (4 tablespoons)

pastured or omega-3 eggs beaten with 1 teaspoon water (2) large square coconut wraps (5)
imported Italian mascarpone (.25 c)
grated Parmigiano-Reggiano (.25 c)

Basil pesto
EVOO (.5 c)
cloves garlic (2)
fresh basil leaves (2 cs)
Parmigiano-Reggiano-crumbled(1-oz.)
pine nuts (.25 c)

For serving
mixed salad greens (5 -oz.)
additional olive oil and balsamic vinegar

Preparation Method:

1. Using a pan, heat your olive oil. Place the spinach in the pan and cook it until it is wilted. This should only take approximately 2 min. When the spinach is done throw it into a separate bowl. Then add mascarpone, and parmigiana, and continue to blend the ingredients together.

2. Line up (2) .5 wraps on your cutting board. Brush the wraps with the egg/water mixture. Using a tablespoon, arrange 4 scoops of filling into the 4 corners of each wrap. Only place 2 on the .5 wrap. Leave an inch or more of space between scoops. Brush another the edge of the alternate wraps with egg wash and place them directly on top of the filled ones. Using your finger press around each scoop of filling to create individual pockets. Then seal the edges with a fork. Using a fluted ravioli cutter, cut out 4 squares. If you do not have a ravioli cutter, a pizza cutter works just as well. Keep the ravioli on the cutting board, to rest, covering them with a linen towel.

3. Using a blender, place all the ingredients for the pesto inside and begin to blend them together. This will make your basil pesto.

4. Using a pan, heat up your left-over EVOO to a medium temp. In small batches, fry the ravioli. This will take approximately 2-3 minutes per ravioli. Remember to flip them when they are halfway done, to ensure an even cooking. Serve with the pesto and salad greens of your choice. Mix your olive oil and balsamic vinegar together and drizzle over the meal.

Fettuccine Alfredo with Fresh Spring Vegetables

Yields: 4 single servings
Phase: 2-3
Cook & Prep: 30 minutes

Ingredients:
sea salt
black pepper
lemon zested(½)
Italian seasoning (.5 teaspoon)
Italian parsley-freshly chopped (.5 c)
EVOO plus more for tossing (.25 c)
box Cappello's fettuccine or 2-3 packs shirataki fettuccine noodles (1)
shiitake mushrooms-sliced(5-oz.)
Parmigiano-Reggiano-grated (.25 c)
asparagus thin trimmed cut into 2-in. sections (1) bunch
Imported Italian mascarpone (1 c)

Preparation Method:

1. Proceed to prepare your pasta according to the instructions as described on the package. Keep 1 cup of the water that you used to cook the noodle for later. Strain out the rest of the water. Using EVOO, toss the pasta in the colander.

2. Using your frying pan, heated to a temp. of medium heat, proceed to heat the EVOO. Toss in some mushrooms and raise the heat to a temperature of medium/high. Then proceed to stir the meal while cooking, for approximately 2 minutes. Add the left-over olive oil, with your asparagus, and .5 teaspoons of salt. Cook, while stirring, until the asparagus is crisp and tender. The mushrooms should be completely browned at this time. This takes around 3 minutes.

3. Turn off the heat and add the mascarpone, along with the cooked noodles. Toss to evenly coat all the ingredients. Next, add your reserved cooking water from your noodles that you previously cooked, .25 cups at a time. Allowing the moisture to thin the sauce and keep the noodles moist. With a gentle motion, stir your herbs, pecorino, lemon zest as well as, Italian seasoning. Flavor with salt and pepper, for taste. Serve immediately.

*Recipe Notes: For those fighting autoimmune disease or strictly in phase 2, it's best to use the shirataki fettuccine noodles instead of the almond flour pasta.

Desserts, snacks, dressings, and drinks

Brussel Sprouts Chips

Yields: 2 single servings
Phase: 2-3
Cook & Prep: 20 min

Ingredients:
Lemon Zest optional
Brussel sprouts outer leaves -2 lbs. of sprouts (2 cs)
melted Ghee (2 tablespoons)
Kosher Salt for flavor

Preparation Method:

1. Heat your oven to a temperature of 350 degrees Fahrenheit.
2. Place the leaves, ghee, and salt into a bowl and mix them together.
3. Once done, layer them, with parchment, on a sheet pan. Separating the leaves into single layers, with no edges touching.
4. Bake the leaves for 10 min, at which time they should be crispy and brown on the edges. Zest some lemon over the leaves and enjoy.

Cinnamon Cassava Flour Pancakes

Yields: 4 single servings
Phase: 1-2-3
Cook & Prep: 35 min

Ingredients:
cassava flour (1 c)
water (.25 c)
monk's fruit sweetener (2 tablespoons)
baking powder (1 tablespoon)
vanilla extract (.5 teaspoon)
eggs room temp. (2) large
nutmeg (,125 teaspoons)
sea salt (.25 teaspoon)
cinnamon plus extra for serving (1 teaspoon)
melted butter plus extra for serving (3 tablespoons)
goat's milk kefir or coconut/almond yogurt, room temp. (.25 c)

Preparation Method:

1. Heat your nonstick griddle to a temperature of medium-low heat.

2. Next, in a bowl, whisk together, sweetener, sea salt, baking powder, flour, cinnamon, and nutmeg, until combined.

3. Then, whisk together, in a different bowl, the water, vanilla, eggs, and kefir/yogurt, until well combined. Whisk the butter in with the kefir mixture.

4. Combine all of the dry mixture with all of the wet mixture, in the larger of the two bowls, continue to whisk, until the ingredients are smooth and well combined.

5. Now, using your .25 measuring cup, scoop the batter and pour it on the griddle that is heated. You can cook up to 3 pancakes at once. Cook them until the bubbles break the surface, and the underside of the pancakes are golden brown. This should be about 2 minutes. Flip them over with a spatula and continue to cook about 1 more minute. Repeat this process with the remaining batter.

6. Serve them immediately or lay them in the oven with the temperature on low, this will keep them warm, until serving. Season with cinnamon and serve with butter.

Vanilla Cake in a Mug in 2-Minutes

Yields: 1 single servings
Phase: 2-3
Cook & Prep: 3 min

Ingredients:
vanilla (.5 teaspoon)
monk fruit sweetener
baking powder (.5 teaspoon)
pastured or omega-3 egg beaten (1) large
EVOO (2 tablespoons)
sea salt-pinch (1)
coconut flour (1 tablespoon)
tiger nuts flour (1 tablespoon)
seasonal fruit or dark chocolate chips (optional
2 teaspoons granular) (1 tablespoon)

Preparation Method:

1. Mix your baking powder, oil, and coconut flour, in a microwave-safe mug. Then, add your tigernut flour, sweetener, salt, and vanilla.

2. Next, add the egg and beat it with a fork until the batter is smooth. Make sure you remember to scrape the sides, As well as, the bottom to blend in all in. This ensures you get all the batter.

3. Gently fold in your fruit or chocolate chips, if you are using them.

4. Place in the microwave and microwave for 1 minute 30 seconds.

5. Let the cake cool for a minute. Then scrape around the inside edges with a butter knife. This will help release the cake from the mug. Shake the muffin out onto a plate. Serve it topped with butter, seasonal fruit, or by itself.

Basil Pesto

Yields: 4 servings
Phase: 2-3
Cook & Prep: 20 min

Ingredients:
parmesan (½ c) fresh grated
pine nuts (⅓ c) toasted
basil leaves (2 cs) fresh
garlic (2) cloves
EVOO (½ c)
Sea salt, for seasoning

Preparation Method:

1. Using a blender place your basil, pine nuts, parmesan, garlic, and a dash of olive oil to pulse the ingredients together. This will make your pesto.

2. Then lower the speed and pour the olive oil in slowly until you have your desired consistency. When you're happy with the texture, turn off the blender. Serve as a dip or with a mushroom cap pizza.

Black Forest Cupcakes

Yields: 18 single servings
Phase: 2-3
Cook & Prep: 1 h 15 min

Ingredients:
Cake
coconut milk (.75 c)
baking soda (.75 teaspoon)
vanilla extract (.5 teaspoon) pure
cassava flour (.75 c)
erythritol or monk fruit sweetener granulated (.5 c)
butter room temp. (.25 c) unsalted
salt (.5 teaspoon)
lemon juice (1 tablespoon)
alternative of vinegar
natural cocoa powder (.333 c)
pasture raised egg (1) large

Filling
prepared espresso (.125 c) (liquid)
butter (.25 c) unsalted room temp
pinch sea salt (1)
black cherries halved pitted (1-pound)
erythritol or monk fruit sweetener (1 c) granulated
Kirschwasser or tart cherry juice (.25 c)

Topping
bitter chocolate shavings (.25 c)
heavy whipping cream (1 c)
erythritol or monk fruit sweetener granulated (1 tablespoon)
Kirschwasser or tart cherry juice .25 teaspoon pure vanilla extract (.5 tablespoon)

Preparation Method:

1. In a separate bowl, set aside 18-20 cherries for decoration for later. Soak the rest in .25 cups of kirsch, until the next day.

2. Heat the oven to a temperature of 350 degrees Fahrenheit. Use oil to grease an 18-cup cupcake baking pan.

3. Next, mix coconut milk, with the vinegar, and allow that mix to sit for 10 minutes.

4. While waiting, using a sieve, sift your cocoa powder, baking soda, flour, and salt, together in a bowl. In a different bowl, that is larger, start to cream your butter and sweeteners until well blended. Then, add eggs to the creamed mix. Alternate between adding dry ingredients and the vinegar-coconut milk to the larger bowl. Making sure to mix the ingredients well.

5. Now, pour your batter evenly, into each cupcake cup. Start with adding one large spoonful and then increase the scoops, as needed. Do not fill the cupcake cups more than 2/3 full. If there is additional batter, use another pan to make more, or work in batches.

6. Place them in the oven and set your timer for 20 min, proceed to bake them. Using a toothpick, inserted into the middle, check to see if it comes out clean. If it comes out clean, then they are done. Cool the cupcakes and then remove them from the pan.

7. Next, start on the filling. Start with beating the butter, until it is creamy and light. Now add in sweetener, espresso, salt, and then mix them together. Making sure the mixture isn't too thick. Add kirsch or cherry juice to thin it out, 1 tablespoon at a time will do.

8. When the cupcakes are done, cut each cupcake in half. Pour 1 teaspoon of kirsch, that the cherries have soaked in, into the bottom half of each cupcake. Then, using a spatula, spread a thin layer of filling, along with a small handful of soaked cherries in between the two halves. Place the top half, of each cupcake, on the layer of filling. This will make a cupcake sandwich.

9. Now prepare your toppings. By placing the crema sweetener, vanilla, and kirsch into a cold bowl, proceed to whip it until it forms peaks.

10. Using a pastry bag, decorate the cupcakes with the cream. Or you could spoon whipped topping onto each cupcake, gently shaping it into a mound to place a cherry on top of. Using a vegetable peeler and a block of chocolate, shred some chocolate on top.
    *Kirschwasser is a cherry brandy.

Lectin Free Blueberry Fools

Yields: 4 single servings
Phase: 2-3
Cook & Prep: 1 h

Ingredients:
organic heavy (1.33 c)
lemon zested as well as, juiced (.5)
blueberries, extra for garnish (2 cs)

real vanilla extract (.5 teaspoon)
pinch of salt
xylitol divided (3 tablespoons)
whipping cream

Preparation Method:

1. Heat up 2 tablespoons of xylitol, 1 .5 cups of blueberries, and the salt, in a boiler over medium heat, until it is bubbly. Lower the temperature to medium/low heat and continue to cook while stirring. The blueberries will be soft when done, approximately 5 min. Take the mixture off of the heat. Next, stir in the lemon zest, and juice and whatever is left of the blueberries. Let it cool to a temperature that is consistent with room temperature.

2. While waiting for the ingredients to cool, beat the vanilla, heavy whipping cream, and remaining tablespoon of xylitol in a mixer, using the whisk attachment. Beat this mixture until you have formed some soft peaks.

3. Now fold the cooled blueberry sauce into the whipped cream. Making sure to be gentle. Next, divide it into separate serving bowls or ramekins. Top it with more blueberries and some chocolate shavings.

4. Enjoy patriotically.

Ginger Cake with Cinnamon and Cream Cheese Frosting

Yields: 12 single servings
Phase: 2
Cook & Prep: 1 h

Ingredients:
Butter Milk
coconut milk (.75 c) unsweetened
Vinegar, apple cider (1 tablespoon) unfiltered raw

Ginger Cake
baking powder (.5 teaspoon)
pumpkin pie spice (2 teaspoons)
baking soda (.75 teaspoon)
eggs pastured (2) large
cassava flour (.75 c)
ground ginger (.5 teaspoon)
granular erythritol (.5 c)
superfine almond flour from blanched almonds (.333 c)
vanilla extract (1 teaspoon) Pure
unsalted butter (.25 c) softened
fine sea salt (.25 teaspoon)
prepared coconut "butter" milk (from step 1)

Icing
cinnamon sticks and cloves for garnish (optional)
butter softened (4-oz.) unsalted
confectioners erythritol (.75 c)
cinnamon for sprinkling
cream cheese (4-oz.) full fat, softened
vanilla extract (1 teaspoon) pure

Preparation Method:

1. Make sure your racks, are centered in the center of your oven, for proper cooking. Warm the oven temperature to 300 degrees Fahrenheit. Using some oil, grease a glass pan that is 9x13-in.

2. Next, mix the Vinegar, apple cider, and coconut milk together in a measuring cup. Then set it aside for later.

3. Start on your ginger cake, by whisking, in your bowl, the baking soda, pumpkin pie spice, flour, ginger, and salt until fully blended.

4. Then, beat your eggs, with your butter, and sugar. Making sure to mix it all together. Now, combine the coconut milk that you created in step 1 and the vanilla, continuing to whisk them to blend them well.

5. Combine the wet mix and dry mix in a larger bowl. Use a spatula to stir, making sure your batter is thick.

6. Now, pour the cake batter into the already greased 9x13 pan. Using a spatula, make sure to spread the batter evenly across the pan. Give the pan a few shakes, to settle the batter into the pan. Do this by shaking it left to right and wiggling it. This is a way to release the air bubbles and settle the batter.

7. Place it in the oven and bake it on the already centered rack, cooking for 40 minutes or until it is completely done. When done, check with a toothpick, by inserting it into the center of the cake, the toothpick should come out clean, with no batter on it.

8. To prepare the icing, you need to beat together the cream cheese, and butter in an electric mixer. Make sure you are using the slow speed on the mixer. As you beat them together, add in the confectioner's erythritol and continue to beat them to get the right consistency. Then pour in your vanilla extract and continue to blend.

9. Your icing should be thin enough to spread with a knife, however, not so thin it drips off your spoon. Check the thickness, if it's too thick, use water, 1 tablespoon at a time

until you reach your desired consistency. This will help to thin out the icing.

10. Now, spoon some of your icing into a pastry bag. By cutting a hole, in one corner of the bag, you can squeeze out the icing. Or wrap cardstock into a funnel and taping it off. Then insert an icing tip into the inside of the funnel, allowing it to stick out at the bottom of the cardstock funnel, you can use this to squeeze out the icing.

11. Proceed to zigzag back and forth over the top of the cake, squeezing the icing out in a zigzag pattern.

12. If you do not have icing tips or bags, then just place a dollop on top of the cake and smooth it with a spatula making sure it is evenly coated.

13. Disperse cinnamon over the top of the cake liberally.

14. Serve the cake in precut squares, with a cinnamon stick and cloves if you like, on top.

*Recipe Notes: This is a great option for a Christmas party or new year's get together.

Peach Cobbler Pancake

Yields: 4 single servings
Phase: 2-3
Cook & Prep: 40 minutes

Ingredients:
baking soda (.25 teaspoon)
vanilla extract (1 teaspoon)
omega-3 or pastured eggs (2) large

tapioca flour (.25 c)
coconut oil (1 tablespoon) melted
cinnamon for sprinkling
coconut flour (.25 c)
liquid stevia (5) drops
goat's milk kefir (5 -oz.)
ripe peaches (2) peeled then cut into paper-thin slivers
cassava flour (.25 c)
fine sea salt (.25 teaspoon)
baking powder (.5 teaspoon)

Preparation Method:

1. In a bowl beat together the eggs, vanilla, stevia, and kefir. Slowly add the coconut oil, whisking constantly, so the oil doesn't solidify.

2. Add the baking powder, coconut flour, cassava flour, tapioca flour, sea salt, and baking soda. Whisking it all together until blended. You should have a smooth, non-lumpy batter.

3. Using a pan pour the batter into single hotcakes. Place a portion of peach slices on as garnish, layering them individually. Sprinkle within cinnamon.

4. Setting the timer for 30 min. bake the cake. When the timer beeps, test whether it is done, by inserting a toothpick in the center of the pancake. If it comes out with no pie filling on it, then you are done. Let the hot cake cool to room temperature before slicing. Serve topped with remaining peach slices.

Arugula-Thyme Pesto

Yields: 4 servings
Phase: 2-3
Cook & Prep: 20 min

Ingredients:
EVOO (.25 c)
baby arugula (1 c) loosely packed
pistachios (.25 c)
clove garlic (1)
thyme leaves (.25 c) fresh

Preparation Method:

1. To make your pesto, using a blender, pulse the garlic, fresh thyme, pistachio, EVOO, and baby arugula until well blended.

2. Then lower the speed and slowly pour in what is left of your olive oil. Blend until you are happy with it, and then turn off the blender.

Ideas for how to eat it:
Over steak or roasted, grilled, or steamed fish
Make your salad dressing: blend (2 tablespoons) waters (.25 c) pesto (2 tablespoons) vinegar red wine, whisking to mix.
Spread on a peeled and de-seeded heirloom tomato half; top with feta

Cilantro-Parsley Pesto

Yields: 4 single servings
Phase: 2-3
Cook & Prep: 20 min

Ingredients:
salt (.5 teaspoon)

EVOO (.25 c)
almonds (2 tablespoon) blanched, sliced
cilantro (1) c loosely packed
lemon juiced (.5)
parsley (1 c) loosely packed flat-leaf

Preparation Method:

1. To make your pesto, using a blender pulse lemon juice, sliced almonds, flat-leaf parsley, cilantro, salt, and a little EVOO until well combined.

2. Then lower the speed and slowly pour in what is left of your EVOO. Turn off the blender when you're happy with the pesto.

Ideas for how to eat it:
With any Mexican food
Make guacamole: mix 2 tablespoons of pesto with 1 avocado, .5 chopped onion, a dash of lime juice, and a pinch of salt
Mixed in with pressure-cooked black beans and cauliflower rice

Sage Pesto

Yields: 4 single servings
Phase: 2
Cook & Prep: 20 min

Ingredients:
sage leaves (1 c) loosely packed
garlic (1) clove
salt (.5 teaspoon)
pine nuts (.25 c) lightly toasted
EVOO (.25 c)

Preparation Method:

1. To make your pesto, using a blender pulse the pine nuts, sage leaves, garlic, salt, and a little olive oil until well combined.

2. Next, lower the speed and slowly pour in what is left of the EVOO. Turn off the blender when you're happy with your pesto.

Ideas for how to eat it:
Over a 20-pound, pasture-raised, oven-roasted Thanksgiving turkey
Make a mustard sauce: mix 2 tablespoon pesto with 1 tablespoon Dijon mustard
In sweet potatoes: Toss 2 peeled, (.25 in) diced sweet potatoes with (.25 c) pesto, (2 tablespoons) maple syrup, season to taste on a baking sheet. Bake 375 degrees, 25 min.

Minty Dessert Pesto

Yields: 4 single servings
Phase: 2-3
Cook & Prep: 20 min

Ingredients:
honey (.25 c)
sliced almonds (.25 c) blanched
mint leaves (1 c) loosely packed
coconut oil (1 tablespoon)

Preparation Method:

1. To make your pesto, using a blender pulse the mint leaves, sliced almonds, coconut oil, and honey until well combined.

2. Then lower the speed and slowly pour in what is left of the EVOO. Turn off the blender when you're happy with the pesto.

Ideas for how to eat it:
Over lamb–minty sweet pairs well with the spicy flavor of lamb
Make a chocolate sauce: Melt .5 c of dark chocolate chips; mix in 2 tablespoons of pesto, pour over coconut milk ice cream (I told you this was adventurous)
Over grilled peaches: Halve and pit yellow peaches, brush with oil, and grill, cut side down, for .5 minutes. Flip and grill 1 minute longer; top with pesto.

Warm Gingerbread in a Mug

Yields: 1 Single serving
Phase: 2
Cook & Prep: 5 minutes

Ingredients:
egg (1) large, lightly beaten
(1) pinch each

- allspice,
- cloves,
- and nutmeg

maple-flavored erythritol syrup (2 teaspoons)
Vinegar, apple cider (.5 teaspoon)
ginger (.5 teaspoon) ground
cinnamon (.25 teaspoon)
butter (1 tablespoon) softened
water (.5 tablespoon)
coconut flour (1 tablespoon)
baking powder (.5 teaspoon)
tiger nuts or cassava flour (1 tablespoon)

Preparation Method:

1. Using a microwave safe mug, beat together the butter, baking powder, cinnamon, coconut flour, tigernut/cassava flour, ginger, and spices.

2. Mix in the syrup, water, cider vinegar, and egg. Beat it vigorously with a fork. The batter should be smooth and consistent. Make sure to clean the sides, by using a spatula to scrape the sides, for any batter, as well as the bottom. This ensures that the batter is well blended.

3. Microwave for 5 minutes. Using a knife cut the edges around the mug to break the muffin free from the mug. Then, shake the muffin out onto a plate. Cut the muffin in half, and top with cinnamon and butter.

Strawberry Short Cake

Yields: 8 single servings
Phase 2
Cook & Prep: 60 minutes

Ingredients:
coconut flour (.333 c)
lemon (.5) grated for zest
baking soda (.75 teaspoon)
arrowroot starch (3 tablespoons)
coconut cream (.5 c) well stirred
Italian butter or French (8 tablespoons) unsalted room temp.
tiger nuts flour (.333 c)

pastured or omega-3 eggs (3) large, room temp.
vanilla extract (.5 teaspoon)
golden monk fruit (.25 c)
fine sea salt (.5 teaspoon)

Whipped Topping
grass fed or organic heavy cream (1 c)
fresh strawberries (1 qt.) hulled and sliced
honey or yacón syrup (1 tablespoon)
vanilla extract (.5 teaspoon)

Preparation Method:

1. Heat your oven to a temperature of 350 degrees Fahrenheit. Using butter, proceed to grease the bottom of a round cake pan, that is 8-in. Using parchment paper, line the pan. Then, grease the pan with another layer of butter and a light sprinkling of flour.

2. Using the immersion mixer, start to beat your butter and sweeteners on high speed. They should become light and fluffy. Using the paddle attachment on medium speed, add the eggs in separately. Next, add the lemon zest, coconut cream, and vanilla extract. Continue to mix well. Scrape whatever batter has rested on the sides of the cup with a spatula making sure to get the bottom of the cup as well. It should be well blended and not lumpy.

3. Sift your flours together: baking soda, coconut flour, arrowroot starch, tiger nut flour, and sea salt. After blended, add it to the butter mix. Proceed to blend it together on a low-speed mixer. It should be smooth when done.

4. Proceed to pour your batter into your greased baking pan. Making sure the cake is smooth, without bubbles. Use a

spatula to smooth the top and tap the pan on the counter. This will help to settle the batter and release air bubbles. Cook the cake and when done insert a toothpick into the center to ensure that the middle is cooked all the way through. The toothpick should come out clean, with no batter on it. This should be 25-30 minutes. Set it to the side, to cool for 30 min. Once cooled, flip your cake onto a rack for further cooling and continue to cool at room temperature.

5. Using a stand mixer, whip the vanilla extract, yacón syrup/honey, and cream in a stand mixer on high speed. Continue to use the whisk and mix until peaks form. Move the room temperature cake to a plate or platter and layer it with whipped topping and then strawberries.

Green Smoothie with Ginger & Mint

Yields: **2 single servings**
Phase: 2-3
Cook & Prep: 20 min

Ingredients:
sparkling water, chilled (16 fluid -oz.)
ice cubes (4)
packed baby greens (2 cs)

- pinch of sea salt
- Chard
- Kale
- spinach

fresh lime juice (1 tablespoon)
avocado (.5)

green banana (1) chopped
ginger root (1 tablespoon) finely chopped fresh
mint leaves (2 tablespoons) packed fresh

Preparation Method:

1. Place everything in a blender, starting with the ice. Then, puree for 1 minute, until it is smooth. Add in additional cold water, to thin, as needed.

Chapter 4: Recipes For The Lectin Free Diet Using The Slow Cooker

Soups and Stews

Cream of Celery Soup

Yields: *4 single servings*
Phase: 2-3
Cook & Prep: 30 min

<u>Ingredients:</u>
Dice celery
Onion * if lectin free omit the onion
celery (1) bunch
sea salt pinch
dill (.5 teaspoon)
water (2 cs)
onion (1) sweet yellow
coconut milk (1 c)

Preparation Method:

1. In the Instant pot add your ingredients. Seal the lid, pressing the soup selection.

2. The soup setting runs for 30 minutes, after that, it goes into automatic *keep warm mode*, for a few hours.

3. After the Instant Pot depressurizes, you can remove the lid. Using your immersion blender, carefully proceed to blend your soup. Making sure that you submerge your immersion blender. This will prevent the hot soup from splattering on you. When it is creamy, the soup is done.

4. Serve immediately.

Pork and Pineapple Stew

Yields: 6 single servings
Phase: 2-3
Cook & Prep: 2 h 10 min

Ingredients:
bacon fat (1 - 2 tablespoon)
coconut aminos (1 tablespoon)
sea salt (½ teaspoon)
stewing pork (2 lb.), 1-inch cubes
ginger powdered (½ teaspoon)
cassava flour (¼ c)
cloves (½ teaspoon) ground
cinnamon (1 teaspoon) ground
turmeric powdered (½ teaspoon)
kumquat jam (2 tablespoon)
pineapple chunks (1 c) bite-sized
garlic (2) large cloves chopped
bay leaf (1)
Alternatives:

- marmalade sugar-free
- Dates

Swiss chard (1) bunch
bone broth (1 c)
onion wedges (1) large

Preparation Method:

1. Marinate your pork cubes with the cassava flour, sea salt, ground cloves, coconut aminos, ginger powder, and turmeric powder for approximately 1 hour.

INSTANT POT METHOD:

1. Using the Sauté function begin to heat the instant pot, until it displays hot.

2. In the pot, place the onions, and fat. Allowing the fat and onions to sauté. Next, throw in your garlic and sauté it.

3. Place the onions and garlic, to the side for later.

4. If you need to add some more oil and proceed to brown your marinated pork cubes in a bowl.

5. Continue by deglazing the bone broth in the pot and set your pork cubes to the side.

6. In your pot place the pork, onion, and garlic. Return the pork, garlic, and onions to the pot.

7. Add in the pineapple, while you are stirring the swiss chards, bay leaf, cinnamon, and kumquat jam.

8. Using the pressure valve, seal the instant pot and set the mode

9. You want to select Meat/ Stew. This should cook for 35 min.

10. When you hear the beep, turn the dial to quick release allowing the pot to vent out the steam.

11. Choose sauté again and add in swiss chard leaves.

12. The leaves should be cooked thoroughly, and the gravy should be super thick. If you need it thicker use arrowroot starch

13. Discard the bay leaf and then season the gravy.

STOVE TOP METHOD:

14. Place a pot over medium heat on your stove and proceed to cook it.

15. Grease the pot with your fat and use it to cook the onions, as well as the garlic.

16. Place the onions and garlic on a plate to the side.

17. Using a bit of oil, start browning your pork cubes in small batches.

18. Once they are browned, set them on the plate with the onions. Use the bone broth to deglaze the pot.

19. Place the pork and onion mix into the pot and continue to cook them.

20. Using a spoon stir the pineapple, cinnamon, swiss chard, bay leaf and kumquat jam until blended.

21. The ingredients should be allowed to boil at this time. Then place a lid on top and let it simmer, with a lower temperature. It should simmer for 45 minutes. Once done the pork should fall apart.

22. Remove your lid and stir with a spoon, make sure to stir in the Swiss chard. Increase your heat and simmer the leaves. The gravy at this time should be thicker.

23. Discard the bay leaves and use salt and pepper for flavor.

24. Serve and enjoy!

*Notes: You can increase or decrease the seasoning as you like.

Butternut Squash Soup

Yield: 4 single servings
Phase: .5/3
Cook & Prep: 45 min

Ingredients:
parsley leaves (.25 c)
butternut squash (1) peeled
onion (1)
cayenne (1 teaspoon)
pepper (.25 Tablespoon)
carrots (3) jumbo
Italian herbs blend (3 Tablespoon)
salt (1 .5 Tablespoon)
celery (2 cs)
garlic cloves (4) peeled
chicken stock (6 c)
coconut milk (1 can) full fat
oregano dry (2 Tablespoon)
chives, fresh
thyme leaves (2 Tablespoon) fresh

Preparation Method:

1. Cut your butternut squash in order to have two, smaller, easier pieces to work with. Using your peeler, peel the butternut squash. Once you have peeled it, trim off the ends. Scoop the seeds out, from the bottom of the squash, with a spoon and toss them in the garbage.

2. Cut your peeled, butternut squash, into large diced pieces, of about the same size.

3. Prep your other veggies. Peel the onions and cut them into large diced pieces. Peel your carrots and cut them into large pieces. Wash your celery and cut them into large pieces. Peel your garlic cloves and chop them.

4. Place the butternut squash, onions, celery, carrots, and garlic into your pressure cooker. Add your thyme and parsley leaves to the pot. using chicken stock, cover the ingredients and then using seasonings, season it.

5. Close your lid on your pressure cooker and begin to cook your soup! On the Instant pot, use the "Soup" function. If you have a manual pressure cooker, you should set the timer to "high pressure" and cook the ingredients for 30 minutes. Once it reaches the appropriate pressure needed, turn the pressure cooker off.

6. Once the instant pot is done, release the pressure with the pressure release valve. Be careful not to burn yourself with the steam!

7. Using an immersion blender or a regular blender, blend your soup until it's completely smooth.

8. Season with oregano, herbs de Provence and cayenne. Add in your coconut milk and stir to blend it all together.

9. Check that it is seasoned, properly.

10. Garnish with fresh chives and enjoy your butternut squash soup.

Slow Cooker Sausage and Zucchini Stew

Yields: 6 single servings
Phase: 2-3
Cook & Prep: 8 h 10 min

Ingredients:
Italian seasoning (1 teaspoon.)
sausage (1 lb.) of your choice
sugar (1 teaspoon.) unrefined
garlic powdered (1 teaspoon.)
celery (2 c) chopped
oregano (1 teaspoon.) dry
(1 teaspoon.) dried basil
onion (1 c) chopped
tomatoes (28 oz.) crushed
salt (1 teaspoon). real
zucchini (3 cs) cut up

Preparation Method:
1. Brown your meat first.
2. Then place all your ingredients into the slow cooker on low.
3. Cook the soup for 6+ hours. Enjoy!

Bone Broth

Yields: 8 single servings

Phase: 2-3
Cook & Prep: 1 h 30 min

Ingredients:
leaks (2) medium
carrot (1) medium
assorted bones (2.5 lbs.)
water (8 cs)
Fish Sauce (2 tablespoons) Red Boat

Preparation Method:

1. Start with dumping your veggies into a pressure cooker and toss in the bones.

2. Next, cover them with water, no more than 2/3 capacity.

3. Now, add in your fish sauce. Cover the instant pot and lock the lid. Program the instant pot to high pressure.

4. Set your time for 2 hours. the more time it cooks, the better it gets.

5. When your bone broth is done, turn the burner off and take the pot off the stove.

6. Let your instant post naturally release the steam. This should only take about 15 minutes.

7. Once done, use a ladle to skim out the fat from on top of your broth, by removing the lid. Using a strainer, pour your broth and allow the chunks to be removed.

Cream Soup

Yields: 4-6 single servings
Phase: 2/3
Cook & Prep: 20 min

Ingredients:
veal bone broth (2 cs)
carrots (1 c) or 2
(6 cs) water
cinnamon (.5 teaspoon)
honey (1 teaspoon)
ripe plantain (2 cs) or 1 medium
Vidalia/ white onion (1 c) or 1, diced
veal-cubed (1-lb)
sea salt (1 teaspoon) divided
basil (.5 teaspoon) dried
broccoli-cut (2 cs) or 1 large florets
white turnips/ rutabagas (2 cs) or 2
coconut flour (.25 c)
garlic (1 tablespoon) or 2 cloves, chopped, peeled
bay leaf (1)
coconut milk (500mL)

Preparation Method:

1. Add 6 cups of water to the instant Pot slow cooker, set it to sauté then allow it to boil.

2. Adding your meat allow it to boil for 3 min. After draining, set it aside.

3. Using some water to rinse your inner pot then place the meat in the instant pot again.

4. Add in the vegetables and veal bone broth, leaving the broccoli out. Season it with cinnamon, sea salt, and herbs.

5. Combine your ingredients by stirring. Now, using the seal setting, cover the pot and set the valve. Selecting the manual button set the timer for 20 minutes.

6. When done use the quick release valve and allow the steam to escape. Remove the meat and veggies once the steam is gone.

7. Before pouring in your coconut milk, set the pot to sauté. Along with some coconut flour, as well as honey. Start to blend it all together.

8. Place your broccoli in and allow it to simmer. This will cook it all the way through. Your gravy should be thicker by now.

9. Toss the bay leaf and the cinnamon stick out, you no longer need them.

10. Join the meat and veggies with the gravy and stir to blend it all together.

11. Use salt and pepper for seasoning.

Best Ever Lectin-Free Chili

Yields: 8 single servings
Phase: 2 meals
Cook & Prep: 6 h 15 min

Ingredients:
sliced scallions & lime wedges for garnish

coconut aminos (2 teaspoons)
avocado oil (1 tablespoon) divided
cumin (2 teaspoons) ground
adobo sauce (1 tablespoon) from preserved chipotles
ground beef (2 lbs.) grass-fed
grass-fed beef broth (2 cs)
garlic (4) cloves, minced
cinnamon (.25 teaspoon) ground
ground cloves (1) pinch
onion (1) medium finely diced
sweet potato puree (1 15-ounce) can
ribs celery (3) finely diced
pine nuts (3-oz.)
chili powder (2 tablespoons)
vinegar red wine (2 teaspoons)

Preparation Method:

1. Using a skillet, heat your oil at a temperature of high. Add in 1-lb of beef and .5 teaspoon of salt. Brown the meat while using a spoon to break up your meat. This can take 4 minutes. Move your meat mix to the Instant Pot and repeat the steps with the left-over beef.

2. Turn your heat down to medium and heat up the left-over teaspoon of olive oil. Add in the garlic, celery, and onion. Set your timer for 5 minutes and allow the ingredients to become soft as they cook.

3. Next, add the cumin, chili powder, cloves along with cinnamon. Stirring while you cook for another minute. Pour in your bone broth. Using a spoon, remove all ingredients from the pan, and place your ingredients into the Instant Pot.

4. Now, add coconut aminos, adobo sauce, wine vinegar, pine nuts, sweet potato puree, 2 teaspoon salt, and pepper for flavor. Using a lid, cover the pot, and place the Slow Cooker on Medium temperature, continue to cook for 6 more hours. Make sure you have the knob, open for ventilation. Top with scallions, lime wedges, and sour cream.

5. Serve and enjoy!

Meats and Meat-based dishes

Keto Bombay Sloppy Joe on Low Carb Buns
Yields: 6 single servings
Phase: 2-3
Cook & Prep: 1 h 15 min
Ingredients:
Carb friendly buns (1) batch

Add-ins One
pistachios (.25 c) shelled
avocado oil (1 tablespoon)

Sauce
water (.75 c)
tomato sauce (1 (15-ounce) can) sugar-free
garlic (1) cloves minced
sea salt (1 teaspoon) grey
avocado oil (2 tablespoons)
garam masala (1 teaspoon), if using turkey or (2 teaspoons) of curry powder, if
using pork
ginger (1 tablespoon) minced
paprika (.5 teaspoon)
Whole chili crushed

Meat
cumin seeds (1 teaspoon)
Whole chili crushed
white onion (.333 c) finely diced,
avocado oil (2 tablespoons)
ground turkey, beef or pork (1-pound)

Add-ins Two
Vinegar, apple cider (1 teaspoon)

coconut milk (.25 c) full-fat
fresh cilantro (small) handful chopped

Preparation Method:

1. Using a pan, place avocado oil and pistachios into the pan and begin to toast them on low/medium heat, for 4-5 minutes. When done, set it aside.

2. In a pot, that is medium in size, add in your avocado oil, warming it to medium. Place your garlic and ginger in the pot browning them for 1 min.

3. Pour your garam masala, chili, tomato sauce, paprika, salt, and water into the instant pot. Cover with a lid, and simmer. Decrease your heat and continue to simmer as it cooks.

4. Add avocado oil and warm it on medium/low heat. Place cumin seeds in, allowing them to toast for a minute. Stir while you add the onions. For 5 minutes sauté the ingredients. Now add chilis and ground beef. The meat should not be pink in the center when done.

5. Place all the cooked meat in with the tomato sauce and let it boil, with the lid covering the pot. Vent the lid, just slightly, to allow the steam to escape. While covered, simmer for 15 minutes with medium/low heat. The mixture thickens as it cooks.

6. Once done, pour in some coconut milk, Vinegar, and toasted pistachios. Using a spoon scoop a large serving of this mix into a gluten-free bun and serve with cilantro as garnish.

One Pot Cranberry Apple Chicken & Cabbage

Yield: 4 single servings
Phase: 2-3
Cook & Prep: 35 minutes

Ingredients:
(1 teaspoon) cinnamon
cabbage (1) small head, shredded & cored
salt (.5 teaspoon) + more, to taste
Vinegar, apple cider (1 tablespoon)
ginger (1 teaspoon) ground maple syrup (1 tablespoon)
cranberries (1 c) fresh or frozen
chicken thighs or breasts (2 lbs.) boneless, skinless
apples (2) cored and sliced
chicken broth (.5 c) (bone broth from the previous recipe)

Instructions:

1. Put all your ingredients, inside your instant pot and proceed to set the timer to poultry. Using the pressure valve, set the lid.
2. Set the timer for 20 minutes.
3. Press the off button, when done.
4. With the natural release, allow it to depressurize for 10 min.
5. Once pressure is gone, open the lid.
6. Serve and enjoy!

Slow Cooker

7. Using a slow cooker, place all ingredients for cooking.
8. Cook the ingredients for 4 hours with the slow cooker on low.
9. Your chicken's internal temperature should be 165 degrees Fahrenheit.
10. Serve and enjoy!

Mango Chicken Thigh Sweet & Sour

Yield: 4 single servings
Phase: 2/3
Cook & Prep: 50 minutes

Ingredients:
cooking fat (1 tablespoon)
honey (2 tablespoons)
chicken thighs (8) deboned
ginger (1- 1") piece, chopped fine
chicken broth (.5 c) or (bone broth from the previous recipe)
fish sauce (1 teaspoon)
red onion (.5) chopped,
green onion (1) sliced (green part only)
mango (1) cut into .5-in. chunks
salt (.5 teaspoon)
cloves garlic (4) chopped
lime (1) juiced
cilantro (.25 c) chopped
coconut aminos (.25 c + 1 tablespoon), divided
Vinegar, apple cider (2 tablespoons) divided

Preparation Method:

1. Press the Sauté button, with the lid off, on the Instant Pot.

2. Place the fat into your pot.

3. Melt the fat.

4. With the skin side down, place your chicken thighs into your pot.

5. Proceed to brown the chicken for around 3 minutes.

6. After flipping the thighs over, brown another 2 minutes. Do 4 thighs at a time.

7. Set the chicken thighs aside for later.

8. Add in onions, mango, and garlic to your pot.

9. Cook until the mangos brown. The onions should be a translucent color when done.

10. Press cancel when you hear the beep. This will turn off your Instant Pot and allow the pressure to release.

11. Nestle the chicken with the mango and continue to cook it.

12. Add in some ginger, cilantro, lime juice, chicken broth, coconut aminos, fish sauce, honey and Vinegar to the pot.

13. Use the poultry button, after placing the lid on the pot. Next, press the pressure button twice to set for high pressure. This sets the time automatically at 15 minutes.

14. When it goes into warming mode, you can turn off the pot.

15. Allow the pressure valve to release the pressure, by turning the knob.

16. Be careful, since the pressure needs to release fully before opening the lid.

17. Set your chicken thighs to the side and finish your recipe.

18. Add in Vinegar, coconut aminos, and some salt to the pot.

19. Use the sauté button to finish cooking.

20. Reduce the sauce down until it is thick.

21. When done, press cancel to turn it off.

22. Serve your chicken thighs with the sauce drizzled over the top.

23. Garnish with slices of green onion.

Lemon and Coconut Chicken

Yields: 4 single servings
Phase: 2-3
Cook & Prep: 30 min

Ingredients:
black pepper (.5 teaspoon) freshly ground
ghee (1 teaspoon) or coconut oil
onion (1) large thinly sliced peeled
fresh lemongrass (1) thick stalk, removing the outer skins, bottoms, and trimming 5 in. off)
kosher salt (1 teaspoon) Diamond Crystal
lime juiced (1)
cilantro (¼ c) fresh chopped
garlic (4) cloves peeled and crushed
coconut milk (1 c) full-fat
ginger (1) thumb-size piece, roughly chopped and peeled
five spice powder (1 teaspoon)
fish sauce (2 tablespoons) Red Boat
drumsticks (10), skin removed

(3 tablespoons) <u>coconut aminos</u>

Preparation Methods:

1. Start with peeling, then trimming, and smashing the lemongrass.

2. Blend your five-spice powder, coconut aminos, lemongrass, garlic, fish sauce, and ginger in a blender. Pour coconut milk in and pulse until blended.

3. Make sure the skin is no longer on the drumsticks.

4. In a bowl, place your chicken drumsticks and begin to season them. Toss the chicken to fully coat them.

5. Plug Instant Pot into your closest outlet and press Sauté, heating your instant pot insides.

6. Melt some ghee or coconut oil in your instant pot with sliced onions. Sauté your onions until translucent, about 5 min.

7. Pour marinade on top of the drumsticks inside the instant pot. Press the Cancel/Warm button and seal the lid in the locked position.

8. Use Manual or Pressure Cook mode and set the timer to 15 minutes, under high pressure. Decrease to 10 minutes, if you have boneless, skinless thighs.

9. When the stew is done, turn the pressure cooker off. Allow the pressure release valve to release the steam. When the pressure drops unlock it and taste your meal.

10. Season with fish sauce or any other seasonings you like.

11. Plate and serve!

Buffalo Chicken Dip With Celery Crockpot Meal

Yields: 4-6 single servings
Phase: 2-3
Cook & Prep: 2 hours

Ingredients:
Cheddar cheese (.5 c) shredded
Cream cheese (8-oz.) Softened
Cooked chicken (1 c) chopped
Hot sauce (.25 c)

Preparation Method:

1. Warm the ingredients in your slow cooker for 2 hours, on low heat, making sure to stir the meal while it is cooking. Once the timer is up, lower the warmth so that you do not overcook the meal and you can keep it warm till you are ready to serve it.

2. Serve and enjoy!

Spicy Black Bean Taco Cs

Yields: 12 single serving cs
Phase 2-3
Cook & Prep: 1h 30 min

Ingredients:
cumin (2 teaspoons) ground
garlic powdered (.25 teaspoon)
Taco cups
water (.25 c) warm
black beans (2 cans) with liquid from the can
onion (.5) medium-finely chopped,
sea salt
oregano (.5 teaspoon) dry
for greasing: olive oil, ghee, or avocado oil
black pepper
coconut aminos (1 teaspoon)
Black Beans Spicy
chili powdered (2 teaspoons)
cassava flour (1 c)
coconut milk (.5 c) unsweetened at room temperature
salted butter (.25 c) melted or palm shortening
coriander (1 teaspoon)
paprika (.5 teaspoon)
avocado oil (1 tablespoon)

Toppings
shredded lettuce
sour cream full fat
goat cheese Cheddar grated
hot sauce
guacamole

Preparation Method:
Taco Cups

1. Turn your temperature to 425 degrees Fahrenheit to preheat the instant pot. Grease the bottom of the muffin pan and sides of a 12-cup muffin tin, with it upside down.

2. Mix together the coconut milk, cassava flour, butter/shortening, and warm water in a bowl until well blended. Separate your dough into approximately (12) 1-oz. balls and roll them out flat. By placing the pieces between parchment, you can make them into small rounds that are 4-in. in size.

3. Peel the dough away from the parchment paper and drape over the underneath of the muffin cups, creating bowls. Folding and pressing the dough to adhere to the cup shape. Bake until golden brown. This should be about 20 minutes. Let them cool, before filling with your desired toppings. Serve.

Spicy Black Beans

4. In a skillet that is nonstick, heated over a temperature of medium/high heat. Stir, the onions placed in your pot, for 2 minutes. Next, pour the coconut aminos along with the spices to flavor the meal. Make sure the onions are fully coated. Stir for 1 minute to coat your onions. Transfer the onions to a pressure cooker, if using a skillet.

5. Add in the black beans and their liquid to your pot, season with sea salt and black pepper to your liking. Pressure cook for another 5 minutes, using high pressure. Allow the steam to naturally release from the pressure cooker. Season with your favorite seasoning of salt/pepper.

6. Using lettuce, fill up your taco cups. Then, the black bean mixture. Top it with goat Cheddar, sour cream, guacamole, and a dash of hot sauce.

*Recipe Notes: Using a Tupperware container you can store your taco cups for a month in the freezer, a week in the fridge, or a few days at room temp. Reheat at 425 degrees Fahrenheit for 10 minutes. If you like them crispier, then prepare the cups in advance and reheat. They will come out crispier.

Seafood, salads, and vegetables

Prosciutto-wrapped Asparagus Canes

Yields: 4-6 single servings
Phase: 2-3
Cook & Prep: 12 min

Ingredients:
Asparagus (1lb) thick
Prosciutto (8oz) thinly sliced

Preparation Method:

1. Add the minimum amount of water and start your pressure cooker.

2. Using the prosciutto, wrap it around the asparagus, making layers of spears along the bottom of your steamer basket. Using unwrapped layers make a plate on the bottom of the basket, preventing sticking and eliminating oil.

3. Then, layer your prosciutto wraps on top in a layer, that is single file. Place your basket inside and proceed to close the lid, while turning your heat up. Once the pan reaches an appropriate pressure, begin to lower the temperature, cooking for 3 minutes on high pressure.

4. Using the normal relief method, open your pressure cooker, allowing the steam to release.

5. Place your ingredients, onto a platter and away from the heat.

6. Serve warm or at room temperature.

Smothered Cajun Greens Recipe

Yield: 4 single servings
Phase: 2-3
Cook & Prep: 35 minutes

Ingredients
garlic (2 teaspoons) (about 2 cloves) crushed
raw greens (6 cups)

- spinach
- onion chopped
- collard
- turnip
- kale
- mustard

salt (.125 teaspoon)
poultry broth (.5 c) or (bone broth from the previous recipe)
turnip (1) chopped
animal fat (1 tablespoon) (I used bacon fat)
uncured ham (1 pound) fully cooked, cut into large chunks

Preparation Method:

1. Place all the components into the cooker.

2. Tightly close your lid.

3. Set your timer to 20 minutes and press your manual button.

4. Using the pressure button, set a high pressure.

5. Turn the instant pot off, when it beeps. That means it is done.

6. Allow, the steam to naturally release for 10 minutes.

7. Using the knob turn it to venting to allow for full pressure release.

8. After all the pressure is released, open your lid safely.

9. Mix the food one last time and serve.

Braised Kale and Carrots

Yields: 2 single servings
Phase: 2-3
Cook & Prep: 30 mins

Ingredients:
Kosher salt
kale (10 -oz.)-roughly chopped
pepper fresh grounds
garlic (5) cloves-roughly chopped & peeled
Aged balsamic vinegar
ghee (1 tablespoon) of or fat of choice
carrots (3) medium cut into ½" slices
chicken broth (½ c) (or vegetable broth if you're feeding vegetarians)
onion (1) medium-thinly sliced

Preparation Method:

1. Get your instant pot out and set it to medium heat. Press the sauté button and proceed to melt your ghee.

2. Sauté your onions, and carrots until they are softened.

3. Toss in the garlic, until it is fragrant, 30 seconds. Place some chicken broth, kale, and seasonings into the pot. Leaving .333 of the space at the top of the stew.

4. Press "Cancel/Keep Warm" and then press "Manual" /"Pressure Cook" button. Next, set your pot for 5 min. under high pressure. Lock your pressure lid, and ensure the valve is pointed towards "Sealing," and go about the day.

5. You can let the pressure drop naturally, which takes 10-15 min, then allow the steam to hiss out by activating the quick release valve.

6. Remove your lid, stir it all to blend, and tastes for accuracy on flavor. Add a splash of balsamic vinegar and if you like, some red pepper flakes for flavor. You can also add a bit of spice if you like to spice it up more.

7. Ladle into individual bowls and serve

Eggplant & Olive Spread

Yields: 4-6 single servings
Phase: 2-3
Cook & Prep: 23 min

Ingredients:
fresh thyme (tablespoon of leaves) a few sprigs of
Fresh EVOO
eggplant (2 lb.) (1k)
lemon (1) juiced
olive oil (4 tablespoons)
salt (1 teaspoon)

tahini (1 tablespoon)
black olives (¼ c) pitted (reserve a few un-pitted for garnish)
water (½ c) (125ml) or (1 c) for electric pots
garlic cloves (3-4), skin on (reserve one to use fresh at the end)

Preparation Method:

1. Using a veggie peeler, make alternating stripes of peel and no peel on your eggplant. Then slice some pretty big chunks to cover the bottom of your pressure cooker, just enough to cover it. Roughly chop the rest of the eggplant.

2. In your pressure cooker, that is preheated, add in the olive oil. Set the pressure to medium heat, before placing the lid.

3. Once the oil is heated, place your largest chunks of eggplant face down and proceed to fry them. They should caramelize on one side, which takes about 5 minutes. Throw garlic and blend it with the eggplant. Sautéing it.

4. Add the uncooked eggplant that is left over and some salt water.

5. Close the lid and lock it. Setting it for 5 minutes.

6. When the time is up, open the instant pot cooker, by releasing the pressure release valve.

7. Carry your pressure cooker base, to your sink and pour the liquid into the sink, to discard of the excess.

8. Using a spoon, scoop out your garlic to remove their skins. Add your Tahini, lemon juice, garlic cloves (cooked as well

as uncooked) and your black olives, proceeding to puree everything together, using your immersion blender.

9. Pour the meal into the serving bowl, then proceed to sprinkle it with some Thyme, and what is left of the black olives. Garnish with fresh olive oil when serving.

Butternut Apple Mash

Yields: 4-6 single servings
Phase: 2-3
Cook & Prep: 20 min

Ingredients:
Primal Palate Apple Pie Spice (.5 teaspoon) or (*AIP see below)
*AIP option replace apple pie spice with (.25 teaspoon) cinnamon and (.125 teaspoon) ginger
apples (2) cored and sliced
butternut squash, (1)
salt (.25 teaspoon) + more to taste
water (1 c)
onion (1) quartered & sliced
Brown Butter, ghee, or coconut oil (2 Tablespoon)

Preparation Method:

1. In your instant pot, pour in your water and insert the steamer basket. Toss the squash, onion, and apples together and place in the basket. Sprinkle with the salt.

2. Seal the Instant Pot and pressure cook it on manual, for 8 minutes. Force release the pressure and transfer the squash mixture to a bowl.

3. Add some brown butter & apple pie spice and fold all ingredients together until well blended.

Steamed Artichokes

Yields: 2 single servings
Phase: 2-3
Cook & Prep: 25 min

Ingredients:
(1 c) water
whole artichokes
(1) lemon wedge

Preparation Method:

1. Cleanse your artichokes with water, removing the damaged leaves. Then use your sharpest knife to carefully trim the stems off. Then proceed to remove a third, of the top half, of the artichoke. To prevent browning, rub the lemon wedges.

2. Place the basket into the instant pot. Lay your artichoke into the pot and pour in water. Ensure that the valve is set when closing the lid. Make sure its sealed to the right position.

3. Press "Manual" mode and your settings on a high pressure. Based on your artichoke size, adjust the temperature: 5 minutes small, 10 minutes medium, 15 minutes large.

4. When time is up, wait 10 more minutes and then release the pressure valve allowing the pressure to release. Use your tongs and place your artichokes on a plate. Watch out they will be hot. Serve them warm with your choice of dipping sauce.

Mashed Acorn Squash

Yields: 4-6 single servings
Phase: 2-3
Cook & Prep: 25 min

Ingredients:
acorn squash (2), seeded, trimmed, halved,
baking soda (.25 teaspoon)
water (.5 c)
salt (1 teaspoon) kosher

Mix in
Salt
brown sugar (2 tablespoon)
pepper
nutmeg (.5 teaspoon) grated
butter (2 tablespoon)

Preparation Method:

1. Place your squash in your pressure cooker. **Then,** season your squash with kosher salt and baking soda.

2. Place the basket or cooking rack in a pot with .5 cups of water, with layers of squash. Pressure lock your lid and increase the pressure cooker to high.

3. Lower your heat so you can keep your setting at high pressure. For 20 minutes, pressure cook your food on a Temperature of high. Use the quick release to allow the pressure to hiss out. Then, place the squash on a plate outside the pressure cooker.

4. Once the squash is cool, scrape the flesh from the squash and place in a bowl. Mix it with brown sugar, nutmeg, as

well as butter. Using a potato masher, proceed to mush them into the butter, allowing it to melt. Your squash should be creamy like mashed potatoes are. There should be no lumps or chunks.
5. Check your mash for consistent flavor and enjoy.

Savoy Cabbage with Cream Sauce

Yields: 4-6 single servings
Phase: 2-3
Cook & Prep: 19 min
Ingredients:
bacon/ lardons diced (1 c)
Savoy cabbage (1) medium head finely chopped (about 2lb)
parsley flakes (2 tablespoons)
onion (1) chopped
mace (¼ teaspoon)
coconut milk (½ can) or 200ml (scant 1 c)
Sea salt, to taste
bone broth (2 cs)
bay leaf (1)

Preparation Method:

1. Prepare your parchment with a pencil, tracing of a circle that is wide enough for the inside ring of the instant pot. Then cut it out with some scissors.

2. Press Sauté, allowing the inner pot to heat to your desired temp.

3. Once it displays the Hot setting, using the inner pot, fry some bacon and onions. Make sure your bacon is crispy. Your onions should look translucent as well as, lightly

browned. Alternatively, change the onions for something more Lectin free. Choosing something from the acceptable vegetable list is fine.

4. Make sure to scoop from the bottom part of your instant pot, to get all the stuck-on bits that have browned and pour the bone broth in.

5. Stir in your bay leaves and cabbage.

6. Cover with your round pieces of parchment and lock your lid. When it reads sealing, you have sealed the valve.

7. Setting your cooking time to 4 min, by selecting 'Manual.

8. When you hear the beep, from your Instant Pot, press 'cancel' setting and allow the pressure valve to release the steam. Making sure all the steam is released and then remove the parchment and uncover the food.

9. Press 'Sauté,' bringing it to a furious boil, adding in mace or nutmeg (whichever you use) along with coconut milk.

10. For 5 minutes, simmering the ingredients before turning the pot off.

11. Garnish with parsley and stir.

12. *Notes: You can also make this meal on the stove in a heavy pot.

Pasta and rice

Cajon Sausage Risotto

Yields: 4-6 servings
Phase: 2-3
Cook & Prep: 30 min

Ingredients:
scallion greens or onions (2 cs) (I don't tolerate onions, so we use the greens (4))
sea salt (1 teaspoon.)
bell peppers, (1½ cs) diced
butter (1 tablespoon)
arborio rice (2 cs)
summer squashes (2) small, diced, seeded, pieces
rope sausage (1½ - 2 lbs.) sliced diagonally, .5 in slices
A handful or two of chopped leafy greens
stock or water (3½ cs)
Cajun seasoning (1 Tablespoon)

Preparation Method:

1. Make your seasoning mixture, by mixing the spices and salt together. Sprinkle the sausage with seasoning.

2. Over a temperature of medium/high, heat your butter in your pressure cooker. Alternatively, if you do not have a pressure cooker, you can cook it in your Instant Pot on sauté. Place some sausage in the pot and cook for 3 minutes.

3. The Sausage should be browned, when done. While stirring, continue to cook for 3 min. or until all the ingredients are ready. Bring the broth to a furious boil.

4. Stir in some rice, greens, squash, bell peppers, scallion greens. Close your lid.

5. Bring the pressure cooker to high, with full pressure. Remove from the heat, after cooking for 5 min. Let the meal sit for 5 min. Allow pressure to release for 3 min.

6. Remove the lid. Stirring to blend and then serve. Top with chopped cilantro and more Cajun seasoning or hot sauce, if desired, for garnish.

7. Be careful, because food out of a pressure cooker is quite hot -it may take a few minutes to cool before it's ready to fork into your mouth! Enjoy!

Eggplant caponata appetizer

Yields: 8 single servings
Phase: 2-3
Cook & Prep: 25 min

Ingredients:
Roma tomatoes (1-pound) diced
vinegar (2 tablespoons) red wine
black pepper (.25 teaspoon)
salt (1 teaspoon)
tomato paste (.5 c), divided
eggplant (1) medium, cut into .5" pieces
zucchinis (2) small cut into .5" pieces
dates (.25 c) chopped
brown sugar (1 tablespoon)
onion (1) small chopped
celery (3) stalks sliced

parsley (.5 c), chopped

Preparation Method:

1. Add all the ingredients, into the pressure cooker, saving ¼ cup tomato paste for later.

2. Set the pressure cooker to 5 minutes. Using the 'Seal' method seal the lid and pressure cook the ingredients.

3. Using the quick release valve, release the pressure and then stir in the leftover .25 cups of tomato paste. Serve it with a selection of flatbread, pita bread, crackers, and olives. Caponata sauce is best served warm or cold, and you can also serve it with pasta noodles and couscous.

Desserts, snacks, and drinks

Pressure Cooker Applesauce

Yields: 4 single servings
Phase: 2-3
Cook & Prep: 30 min

Ingredients:
apple juice (.5 c)
apples (12) medium-diced, cored (peeled if preferred)

Preparation Method:

1. Start by chopping your apples into pieces. Then place your apples in the inner pot of your Instant Pot.

2. Next, add in your apple juice, this will help you keep the apples from getting dry and also helps you make the applesauce.

3. Using scissors, cut a circle out of parchment that is large enough for the inside of the instant pots inner rim, and then place it over your apples. This helps the heat and the apples stay good in the pot.

4. Using the sealing method, cover with a lid and seal the pot, so that the apples can be pressurized.

5. Adjusting your cook time, to 10 minutes press 'Manual' setting. And allow the apples to cook down.

6. As soon as the cooking time is over and the pressure cooker beeps, release the pressure naturally, as to let the steam out. Be careful and make sure that you do not burn yourself.

7. Uncover the apples and discard the parchment paper circle in the trash. You will no longer need this.

8. Using an immersion hand mixer, blend the apples until they are smooth, and it creates an applesauce, that is the proper consistency.

9. Serve and enjoy!

*Notes: The applesauce will taste sweeter if you use apple juice and or non-alcoholic cider.

Paleo Yogurt

Yields: 4 single servings
Phase: 2-3
Cook & Prep: 25 min

Ingredients:
honey (2 Tablespoon.) raw
yogurt extra thick
vanilla extract (1 teaspoon.)
capsules of probiotics (2), or yogurt (2 Tablespoon.) previously made
coconut milk (2 (13.5 oz.) cans) full fat, or use coconut cream (1 (33 oz.) box)

Preparation Method:

1. In the fridge, cool the coconut milk or cream, at least 6 hours (or overnight). The milk will separate from the cream, this is okay.

2. Once you open the can or box, scrape the cream into a bowl.

3. Hint: Open from the bottom. Then pour milk into another container and proceed to scrape the cream out. Save the milk for smoothies.

4. Add in 2 tablespoons of yogurt or 2 capsules of probiotics, broke open. Pour in honey and vanilla for flavor. Proceed to blend it by hand, until well blended.

5. Divide between glass jars, without lids and place in your yogurt maker. Following the instructions of the machine.

Let it sit for 15-20 hours. More fermentation time makes the flavor sourer.

6. Place the sealed jars into the fridge, for hours to cool. Yogurt, sealed in the fridge, keeps for 2 weeks.

*Tip: It is normal for your yogurt to settle when in the fridge, just stir and enjoy.

Candied Chickpea Cajun Trail Mix

Yields: 5 single servings cups
Phase: 2-3
Cook & Prep: 17 min

Ingredients:
mango (6-oz.) regular dried or spicy chili dried mango to add after (if desired)
tablespoon of water
ginger pinch ground
cashews (.33 to .5 c)
sea salt pinch
pecans (1 .5 cs) raw halves
almonds (1 c) raw
spicy Cajun seasoning or mix (.5 to 1 tablespoon)
maple syrup (.5 c) pure
butter (2-3 tablespoon) or nondairy (vegan) butter
chickpeas (1 c) or more (10 -oz.) drained
sunflower seeds (.25 c) raw

Preparation Method:

1. Place all your ingredients, minus the butter, into your Instant Pot. Mix it thoroughly.

2. Sauté with a plastic spatula, until the butter is all melted, and the nuts/ chickpeas are fully coated with the seasoning

and the maple syrup. If the batter seems too sticky/thick once sautéing, add an additional 1 tablespoon of water.

3. Switch to the pressure cooker and place it on 'Manual' cooking mode for 10 minutes.

4. Use the 'Quick Release' valve once the timer is done.

5. Remove it from the pot & spread the nut mix, onto a lined cooking sheet. Bake it on 375 degrees Fahrenheit for 7-10 minutes; making sure to turn the nuts/seeds halfway through cooking. Any longer might burn the nuts. The chickpeas will be a little less cooked, but still tasty!

6. Remove them from the oven and Let the Cajun trail mix sit and completely cool.

7. Finally, dice your mango into tiny, small pieces. Then, add them to your candied Cajun trail mix and stir it all together. It's easiest to do this in a large ziplock or airtight container. If you are using plain dried mango, feel free to add more spices to the mix to evenly coat the nuts.

8. Store it in a sealed container.

Note You can use a slow cooker if you do not have an instant pot. The trail mix method follows the same recipe but eliminates the oven part. To ensure that your nuts don't burn, keep an eye on the cooking times.

You can make this even more paleo friendly, by removing the chickpeas.

If want crispier chickpeas, try adding in some roasted chickpeas, after cooking, instead of cooking the canned ones.

Classic Hummus

Yields: 18 single servings
Phase: 2-3
Cook & Prep: 1 h 49 min

Ingredients:
salt (.5 teaspoon)
garbanzo beans (.5-pound) dry
water (3 .5 c) (for cooking beans)
granulated garlic/ garlic powder (.5 teaspoon)

For the Hummus
Optional for garnish:

- olive oil
- oregano
- paprika

peppers (.25 teaspoon) drained, cooked garbanzo beans
olive oil (2 Tablespoon)
reserved cooking liquid (.75 c)
tahini (.333 c)
garlic clove (1) fresh chopped roughly
salt (.75 teaspoon)
cumin (.25 teaspoon)
lemon (.5) zested
whole lemon juiced (1)

Preparation Method:
Cooking the Beans

1. Add in some water, garlic powder, dry beans, and salt to the Instant Pot.

2. Close the lid of the instant pot, lock it and begin to cook on manual mode at high pressure for 60 minutes, with a full natural pressure release.

3. Drain the beans in the sink and save the cooking liquid to use in the hummus. Next, allow them to cool for a couple of minutes. It's okay if they are still slightly warm, but you don't want them to be piping hot.

Making the Hummus

1. Add the cooked beans, along with a half cup of cooking liquid, tahini, lemon juice, lemon zest, pepper, olive oil, salt and cumin to the food processor, and blend.
2. Stop the food processor and check the flavor as well as, consistency of your hummus. Add in more cooking liquid, if desired. Use roughly a total of (.75 c) of cooking liquid.
3. Serve and enjoy! Refrigerate leftovers for up to a week.

Paleo Banana Bread

Yields 4-6 single servings
Phase: 2-3
Cook & Prep: 35 min

Ingredients:
cassava flour (1 .5 c)
baking soda (.5 teaspoon) ghee (.33 c) softened
baking powder (1 teaspoon)
cashew milk (,33 c) (or coconut, almond, etc.)
vanilla (1 teaspoon)
coconut sugar (.75 c)
egg (1) (room temperature)
salt pinch
cream of tartar (1 .5 teaspoon)

bananas (2) mashed, very ripe

Preparation Method:

1. *Buttermilk*: in a bowl place your milk and cream of tartar, allowing it to curdle. This creates the buttermilk.

2. Place the butter, with the sugar, and cream it together. Add vanilla and eggs, then blend well.

3. Continue mixing, while adding in bananas, that are mashed.

4. In a bowl, mix baking soda, baking powder, cassava flour, along with a pinch of salt.

5. Then, begin to mix in the wet ingredients, gradually.

6. Pour in the buttermilk, made earlier.

7. Using foil, cover with a "tent" and spray with oil spray. This prevents sticking.

8. Grease a 7-inch dish and add in the mix.

9. In the instant pot, add in 2 cups of water.

10. In the bottom of the instant pot, set the trivet.

11. Place your pan with batter onto the trivet.

12. Pressure seal the lid.

13. Press MANUAL on high, for 30 minutes. It will count down until it reaches, the appropriate pressure.

14. When your Instant Pot beeps, allow it to NATURALLY release the steam, being careful, making sure the tin doesn't burn you. This takes 17 minutes roughly.

15. Remove the lid, when the pressure releases fully.

16. Being careful remove your trivet and pan. Take off the foil and place on a wire rack to let it cool.

17. When done cooling, remove and take it out of the pan.

18. Enjoy with some coffee.

Coconut Milk Yogurt

Yields: 4 single servings
Phase: 1- 2-3
Cook & Prep: 12 hours

Ingredients:
Aroy-D coconut cream (1 (33.8 oz) carton)
Seeking Health ProBiota Sensitive probiotics* (2) capsules
gelatin (1 tablespoon) Great Lakes (red can)

Preparation Method:

1. This recipe takes 13 hours, so be available when it is done.

2. Starting first thing in the morning is ideal since it should be done that night. Plug in your Instant Pot, shake your coconut milk and pour it into the pot.

3. Seal your instant pot lid and set it to YOGURT, press the "adjust" setting, so the button says "boil." You should be boiling/scalding your milk to kill off any of the bad bacteria., which allows for you to replace it with good bacteria.

4. If the instant pot beeps, it is signaling that it is completed. It is ready to cool so that you can continue on to the next step. Set it aside and allow it plenty of time to cool.

5. The milk should cool below 115 degrees Fahrenheit, which you can check, using a meat thermometer to gauge the temperature. After it is cool, empty your probiotics into the milk, allowing the good bacteria's to grow. Whisk it vigorously, to blend.

6. Return the reservoir to your instant pot and pressure seal the lid. Press the YOGURT button and the "+" to set the time to 12 hours, which will give you a great amount of tartness.

7. After 12 hours, the machine will beep, signaling that it is done. After this, make sure you have reached the appropriate sourness. If it is not the right flavor for you, then place it back on for 12 more hours, with 2 more probiotic capsules.

8. Sometimes you will receive capsules, that are no-good, that is ok. Just start from the probiotics stage again and heat for 12 more hours.

9. If it is to your liking, take out the reservoir from the instant pot. Using some gelatin, dispense it over the top evenly, and begin to whisk until well blended. The gelatin should be well blended, with no lumps that are visible.

10. Separate out, your desired amount of servings per container. Then place them into the fridge, to cool and set, for several hours. This is best done overnight, to allow the yogurt to fully set. Be patient, it will make a difference.

11. *Optional:* You can pour in sweeteners or any flavor choices you like before placing it into the fridge to set. This will add flavor and texture to the yogurt. Some good choices are maple syrup, vanilla, melted honey, coconut sugar, etc. Play around with the flavors and add-ins, making it your own recipe.

Strawberry-Balsamic Sauce

Yields: 2 single servings
Phase: 2-3
Cook & Prep:

Ingredients:
balsamic vinegar (2 tablespoons)
organic honey (.25 c) (or to taste) raw, or any honey will do.

strawberries (1 (16 oz.)) bag of frozen
water (.25 c)

Preparation Method:

1. Get your smallest saucepan out and heat it at low heat, with your strawberries and water to make a glaze. Cook it down to melt the strawberries and make it soft and glaze-like.

2. In that same saucepan add in the balsamic vinegar, and honey, continue cooking for 15 minutes. Then use an immersion mixer and blend it all together until it is all smooth.

3. Continue cooking over a temperature of medium heat, the sauce should begin to thicken. Continue stirring, allowing the sauce to reach the desired consistency. Then, you want to scoop the sauce into one, big mason jar and seal it. Place the sauce into the fridge until it is cool and ready to serve.

4. You can serve on any cakes, pastries, muffins, or over breads. It is also a delicious treat in your yogurt, which you previously made. It's great with pancakes, as a jam or over non-dairy ice cream.

Conclusion

Thank you for making it through to the end of *Lectin Free Diet*, let's hope it was informative and able to provide you with all of the tools you need to achieve your goals whatever they may be.

The next step is to start the three phases of the Lectin Free Diet. Each phase is designed to help you heal your gut and alleviate the symptoms of your autoimmune disorders. Lectin is harmful to our bodies. It is contributing to the mass diagnosis of autoimmune disorders. When you continue to eat lectin in your diet, you are not allowing your gut to heal, from the previous dose of lectin, that you took consumed earlier. Our guts are designed to heal themselves, but by eating lectin in most of our foods, we are not giving our gut time to digest properly or heal properly. Irritable bowel syndrome is another symptom that can be alleviated by eliminating the lectin from your diet. Take the first step in alleviating your gut issues and remove lectin from your diet. Then come back to our Amazon page and let us know how this diet has helped you with your health.

Finally, if you found this book useful in any way, a review on Amazon is always appreciated!

Made in the USA
Lexington, KY
26 April 2019